To Michelle

"I had to read this book through in a single sitting because it pulled me through from start to finish. This will be a valuable contribution to our growing understanding of church-planting movements and their history, scope and nature. I will be recommending this to everyone I know."

**DAVID GARRISON,** International Mission Board, Southern Baptist Convention

"'Adaptive, innovative and consuming.' Those words characterize the movements Steve Addison describes and prescribes in his book. They also depict the book—pick it up and it won't let go of you. I couldn't put it down till it finished rearranging my mind. This is a keeper!"

**RALPH MOORE,** author of *How to Multiply Your Church*

"In this book Steve Addison demonstrates the desire of God from the biblical era until today. He casts a compelling future vision by tracing God's discernible lessons demonstrated in movements. Steve taps into the heart hunger of the growing number of us that want to see God do something great. Your heart will be stirred while you read *Movements That Change the World*. If you are like me, you will be prompted to stop and pray, 'Lord, do it again, for the sake of our communities and nations—for every man, woman and child!'"

**ED STETZER,** author of *Planting Missional Churches*

"I love this book! Every so often a book comes along that fuels the flame that was started in my heart years ago when I was a young and on-fire world changer. I love reading this type of book. I'm still a fanatical, fiercely focused, imbalanced, apostolic type guy. I'm older now, but more fervent than ever. If you're looking for an intelligent and passionate book to stir you to dream big dreams of how a movement can begin through your life and that will give you practical tools to help implement those dreams, then read *Movements That Change the World!*"

**FLOYD MCCLUNG,** author of *You See Bones, I See an Army: Changing the Way We Do Church*

"There are very few who have truly studied, dissected and understood church multiplication movements at the core. My friend Steve Addison has done his homework. I have anticipated this work for some time and am pleased to report it is better than I ever expected. Steve has put in the years of research and synthesizes his vast amounts of experience, wisdom and research into an easy-to-read book."

**NEIL COLE,** founder of Church Multiplication Associates and author of *Organic Church*

"Steve has been tantalizing me with tales of this book for years. He has talked to me about the content on numerous occasions. The chapters are distilled from years of experience and thought, and the final product has not disappointed. Practitioners and thinkers with a passion for mission will want to read and reread this book."

**MARTIN ROBINSON,** director of Together in Mission, UK

"An important book for our times—well researched, well written and well thought out. Steve identifies the essential qualities that have defined movements of the Spirit throughout the ages. The stories he tells—biblical, historical, contemporary and personal—give us hope for fresh movements of God in our day."

**ROBERT E. LOGAN,** CoachNet International Ministries

# Movements That Change the World

## Five Keys to Spreading the Gospel

## Steve Addison

Forewords by Alan Hirsch and Bob Roberts Jr.

IVP Books

An imprint of InterVarsity Press
Downers Grove, Illinois

InterVarsity Press
P.O. Box 1400, Downers Grove, IL 60515-1426
World Wide Web: www.ivpress.com
E-mail: email@ivpress.com

Revised edition © 2011 by Steve Addison
First edition © 2009 by Steve Addison

First edition printed in the United States 2009 by Missional Press.

The map on p. 53 is from Todd M. Johnson and Sun Young Chung, "Tracking Global Christianity's Statistical Center of Gravity, A.D. 33- A.D. 2100," International Review of Mission 93 (April 2004): 166-81. Used by permission.

Every effort has been made to trace and contact copyright holders for additional materials quoted in this book. The author will be pleased to rectify any omissions in future editions if notified by the copyright holders.

While all stories in this book are true, some names and identifying information in this book have been changed to protect the privacy of the individuals involved.

Design: Cindy Kiple

ISBN 978-0-8308-3619-2

Printed in the United States of America ∞

**Library of Congress Cataloging-in-Publication Data**

Addison, Steve
    Movements that change the world: five keys to the expansion of Christianity/Steve Addison.
        p. cm.
    Originally published: Missional Press, c2009.
    Includes bibliographical references.
    ISBN 978-0-8308-3619-2 (pbk.: alk. paper)
    1. Missions—History. I. Title.
BV2100.A33 2011
266.009—dc22

                                                                2010040610

P   18   17   16   15   14   13   12   11   10   9   8   7   6   5   4   3   2

Y   26   25   24   23   22   21   20   19   18   17   16   15   14   13   12

*These men have caused trouble all over the world.*

ACTS 17:6

# Contents

# Foreword

**S**teve and I go a long way back. We shared many of the same classes in seminary. It soon became clear that we also shared a passion for the idea of movements and their relevance for mission today. As we met over the years, we have shared many ideas that we think are vital to recover in our day if we are going to reverse the decline of the church at the dawn of the twenty-first century. The result has been one of the most theologically fertile friendships that I have ever had. We have argued some, agreed mostly, and refined our thinking all the time, but definitely we have mutually enriched each other's views on this vital topic over the last twenty years. Steve's friendship has been a kind of mentorship that has left me a much richer person, for which I am profoundly thankful. His influence can be found throughout my own writings on this topic.

Steve brings a passionate love for God and his people to the task of writing. In *Movements that Change the World* you will discover an engaging description of the dynamics of missionary movements and how to initiate, maintain and extend them. Behind this unencumbered, nontechnical portrayal of the examples of history and their ongoing witness lies a lifetime of research that brings together disparate insights from theology, church history, sociology, business studies, missiology, leadership studies, spirituality and everything in between. This book is a labor of love that has taken decades of service to prepare.

Instructed by the lessons of history, fueled by a missionary's vision of what the world can be, and guided by deep commitment to orthodox, historic Christianity, this book should be read by all who wish to rediscover what it means for Christianity to be a missional movement again in the West.

*Alan Hirsch*

# Foreword

I had the privilege of meeting Steve for the first time in 2008 at a small global gathering of influential pastors who had all planted churches and were planting churches out of their existing churches. I've followed Steve's blog and writings for years, and I'm delighted he has gathered his insights into book form. Studying church planting movements is challenging because of all the history, facts and contexts—it isn't easy work, and sometimes it is not easy work to read! That's where Steve comes in.

Steve has done his homework and has all the academic qualifications necessary to identify the five core characteristics of a church planting movement—maybe any movement. The good news is he does this in a way that enables all of us, not just the academics, to understand it. After all, it's going to be our "everyday disciples" who will make this happen. He then gives both historical and contemporary examples to illustrate how it works.

The character and experiences of the book's author are huge in terms of how much you can trust what's written. That is another point where Steve really stands out. He lives this stuff. He has planted churches, been involved and is recognized as one of the top global leaders in training church planters. He is also a student and researcher of church planting and movements.

I not only endorse this book but also will require all of our interns, students and residents to read it. Thanks, Steve, for a great gift to the body of Christ!

*Bob Roberts Jr.*

# Acknowledgments

It was about twenty years ago that I became fascinated with movements and discovered my calling was to fuel church planting movements. It has been a long, hard road to get to the place of readiness to write this book—hard, but good. God is faithful, and along the way he has brought so many people into my life who have helped me go the distance.

To Peter Costello, Bill Hallam, Pete Fitzgerald, Nigel Barr, Rod Denton, Terry Walling, Rick Paynter, Bob Logan, Sam Metcalf, Andrew Herbert, Alan Hirsch, Craig Winkler and Buck Rogers— thank you.

Thanks also to Patrick Innes and Rod Smith who walked with me through the dark days of 2007. Thanks also to Val Gresham, my writing coach and editor; to David Phillips, who saw the potential of this project; and to Alister Cameron, my blogologist. Finally I'd like to thank IVP for the opportunity to make the book available to a wider audience.

Dad, thanks for your example of Christian leadership and, even more, for your commitment to Mum right to the end.

Michelle, you are my one and only love. You stood by me and never stopped believing in God's call on my life. Thank you.

# Patrick

*I, Patrick, a sinner, unlearned, resident in Ireland, declare myself to be a bishop. Most assuredly I believe that what I am I have received from God. And so I live among barbarians, a stranger and exile for the love of God. He is witness that this is so.*

PATRICK, IN A LETTER TO COROTICUS

**W**hen Alaric and his army of Visigoths marched into Rome to loot and plunder in A.D. 410, it was as though the world had ended.[1] It had been eight hundred years since an enemy last breached the defenses of Rome—the Eternal City, the heart and soul of the greatest empire in history.

The sack of Rome sent a shock wave throughout the Empire. Yet it was hardly noticed on the Empire's fringes—except perhaps by the Irish pirates who for years had been taking advantage of the withdrawal of the Roman navy to attack the west coast of Britain.

Patrick was sixteen years old when Irish raiders stormed his village in Roman Britain.[2] Until that day he had lived a privileged life. He was born into the British landowning aristocracy. His grandfather was a priest, and his father was a magistrate and church leader. The life of a Roman magistrate was one of honor

and privilege. The position was hereditary; one day Patrick would
rule as part of Roman nobility in Britain. The raiders seized him,
along with servants from his father's estate, and returned across
the sea to the pagan land of Ireland, where they sold him into
slavery. The year was A.D. 405.

For the next six years Patrick lived the lonely and hard life of a
slave, working as a shepherd. Isolation, hunger and cold brought
him misery, and misery taught him humility. God worked power-
fully in Patrick's suffering to remake him from the inside out. He
freed Patrick from dependence on wealth and his place in society.
God rescued Patrick from himself and made his heart captive to
the love of Christ.

According to Patrick, before his abduction he did not believe in
the living God. As a slave, Patrick came to see the hand of God in
his troubles. God broke through his defenses, and Patrick faced
his unbelief and pride. Later he described how he turned to God,
who he realized had been watching over him all the time. He became aware of God's protection, and he discovered that God loved
him as a father loves his son.

Outwardly nothing changed for Patrick; he was still a captive in
a harsh foreign land, but he saw life differently. The land of his
captivity had become the land of his freedom in God. The slave of
men had become a son of God.

The love and fear of God grew in him. Patrick learned to pray
continually as he worked. At night he stayed out in the forests and
on the mountains to pray. He would rise before dawn to pray in
the icy coldness of the Irish winter. This was no burden to him but
a delight; the Spirit was burning in him.

One night God spoke to him in a dream and revealed that there
was a ship waiting to take him home. There was one problem—
two hundred miles of dangerous territory lay between him and
the coast. Patrick made his escape and began the long journey
home as a runaway slave.

The details are sketchy, but he reached the ship and eventually made it back to his family and resumed the life he once had in Britain. Perhaps he looked forward to inheriting his father's position in society and all the privileges that went with it. But God, who is the initiator in this story, had other plans for Patrick.

Patrick woke one night to the voices of the people he had known in Ireland crying out, "We beg you, come and walk with us again!" Their cry pierced his heart. God was calling him to return—and he did.

In time, despite his limited education and experience, he was ordained as a priest and bishop. Later Patrick faced opposition to his authority from church leaders, but he believed that it was God who had appointed him, an uneducated sinner, to be a missionary bishop to the Irish.

When Patrick returned to Ireland, it had been four hundred years since Christ commanded his disciples to go to the nations, yet the gospel was largely contained within the borders of the Roman Empire.[3] God took the initiative to transform a teenager with an inherited faith into an apostle compelled by the Spirit to take the gospel to the ends of the earth. The shepherd-boy slave had become the slave of Christ and apostle to Ireland.

Patrick's troubles had prepared him well for his mission. Through them he had become devoted to Christ and the gospel. His heart longed to reach the "barbarians" beyond the borders of civilization. His lack of formal training contributed to his openness to new and effective methods.

In contrast, the church of the Roman Empire was not interested in taking the gospel beyond the borders of Greco-Roman civilization. Romans regarded the tribes outside the Empire, such as the Celts, the Goths and the Huns, as barbarians. The religious world of the Irish Celts was inhabited by a bewildering array of gods, goddesses, and spirits of the sky, earth and water; the Celts also believed in the magical powers of ancestors and divine animals.[4]

For the church of the Roman Empire, these pagan barbarians were beyond the missionary concern of God.

Patrick, however, saw the need and opportunity to reach these Irish barbarians. He traveled throughout Ireland to remote and dangerous places to preach, baptize converts and ordain clergy for the new churches. From nobles to slaves, the Irish were ready to hear and obey the gospel. Thousands of them responded to Patrick's preaching and turned from their pagan idols to serve the living God. Many of the converts took up Patrick's challenge to join his missionary band.

Steadily the gospel worked its power through the Irish tribal society. Patrick embraced the best of Celtic culture and redeemed it to serve the gospel. He fought those aspects of Irish culture that did not conform to the gospel. He ended the slave trade, and under the gospel's influence, murder and tribal warfare decreased. In place of a warrior society, Patrick provided a living alternative, showing the Irish that it was possible to be brave—to expect every day to be murdered, betrayed, enslaved—and yet to be people of peace with no fear of death because of the promises of an almighty God.[5]

Patrick faced fierce opposition. He had to contend with the magic of the Druids (the powerful priestly caste of Celtic society), and he faced the violence of local chieftains. On one occasion, newly baptized Christians were attacked by British raiders from the west coast of Patrick's homeland. The men were slaughtered, and the women and children were kidnapped, some of them still wearing their baptismal robes.

Just as distressing was the opposition from other church leaders. Patrick's writings make it clear that influential sections of the church disapproved of him, despite his role in the conversion of much of Ireland.[6] Patrick's worst critics were the bishops in Britain. Not interested themselves in taking the gospel to the Irish, they may have initially tolerated the appointment of such a poorly educated novice; but as the Christian faith spread throughout Ireland some church leaders questioned whether Patrick was the right person to lead such a successful and potentially lucrative ministry.[7]

Patrick was deeply conscious that his authority to preach the gospel came from God, but he was also painfully aware of his limitations and of his many critics. He was embarrassed by his lack of formal theological training and the poor quality of his Latin. His writings do not reveal the training of a scholar, but they do reveal the heart of a man compelled by the love of Christ, led by the Spirit and guided by the Scriptures.[8]

Patrick gave the Irish the gift of non-Roman Christianity. Since the conversion of Emperor Constantine in A.D. 312, Christianity had been closely identified with Roman culture and power. Yet Patrick liberated Ireland without the backing of imperial power. Instead he lived and communicated the gospel in ways that connected and resonated deeply with Irish hopes and concerns. He taught the Irish that they could become followers of Christ without having to become like Romans.

Patrick made church structures serve his mission. The church of the Roman Empire was based around the cities where the local bishop was supreme. The Irish were a rural and tribal people. Unlike the civilized Romans, they had no settled towns, roads, currency, written law, government bureaucracy or taxation. Irish society was decentralized and organized around tribes led by local "kings."[9] So Patrick decentralized the church.

The Roman system was based on the diocese and the bishop. The life of the Celtic church revolved around the monastery, which was led by an abbot. The abbots selected the bishops, and the bishops were dependent on them.

Patrick's mobile missionary bands closely followed the example of Jesus and Paul, but the Roman church leaders did not approve. Patrick responded to his critics through his writings as best he could with his limited literary skills, but he did not let them stop him. Not only was his ministry at stake, but also the missionary movement that was about to be unleashed throughout Britain and Europe.

The Celtic missionary movement was not a highly organized or centrally controlled operation. Under Patrick's influence, wave after wave of Irish youth flooded into monastic life. Most monasteries began in remote places when their founders withdrew from the world only to be pursued by throngs of young men who were eager to follow their example.[10] Monastic founders responded to the call of Christ and gathered workers around them. Each founder developed his own Rule for his followers.[11]

The monasteries were places of spiritual devotion and learning, but they were also sending centers. The Irish church took on the character of a missionary movement. For centuries Ireland became a base from which Christianity spread throughout the British Isles and to much of western and northern Europe as monks followed the call to "go pilgrimage for Christ."[12]

Patrick's followers shared a love for classical literature and the pagan poets, but the Scriptures had first place in their hearts and minds.[13] They read them with passion rather than detached academic interest. Although few were great theologians, they were known for their spiritual authority and missionary zeal. Young men who once would have given their lives in feuds between the clans now gave their lives to plant the gospel wherever Christ led them.

Under the abbot, each missionary outpost made decisions in adapting to local needs and opportunities. They recruited new missionaries from the local people and sent them out to found new monasteries.[14] This made Celtic monasticism highly flexible, adaptable and transplantable—everything that the church of the Roman Empire was not.

Since Ireland had no cities, the rapidly growing monasteries became the first population centers—hubs of unprecedented prosperity, art and learning.[15] A distinct Celtic Christian culture emerged. For hundreds of years missionaries and scholars went out from Ireland, while students from many lands came to Ireland and left inspired to become missionaries. These missionary monks founded the monasteries throughout Europe that would one day become great cities.[16] Patrick's personal achievements were impressive, but this missionary movement, inspired by him, is his greater legacy.

The Celtic missionary movement continued to be shaped by Irish monk Columba (521-597), whose grandfather had been baptized by Patrick. Sharing Patrick's commitment to the Bible, love for Christ and missionary zeal, Columba and twelve companions left Ireland for the island of Iona off the coast of Scotland. There Columba established a missionary base for the evangelization of the pagan Scots and Picts. For centuries Iona served as a center for training and sending out missionaries and the establishment of other sending centers throughout Ireland, Scotland and northern England.

As the number of monasteries multiplied throughout Ireland, Britain and the European continent, converts were won and new missionaries left to "go pilgrimage for Christ" wherever they felt his leading. These monasteries became dynamic centers of spiritual devotion, learning, industry and evangelism in a chaotic world.

What part did the Roman church play in this story? Rome was the center of civil and ecclesiastical power. The Roman church had a distinguished history stretching back to the apostles. It had built efficient organizational systems throughout the empire, and it had money and clout. Yet the Roman church was strangely absent from the frontline of missionary expansion.

As the Roman Empire and civilization collapsed, it was not the Roman church but the church of the barbarian Celts that led the way in missionary endeavor and cultural transformation. The Celts had biblical simplicity and devotion to Christ on their side. They shaped their church structures and methods to fit their culture and missionary purpose. Rome had the resources, but the followers of Patrick had the zeal.

Patrick died in 461. As the western part of the Roman Empire crumbled and darkness spread over much of Europe, the light of the gospel continued to shine brightly from remote Ireland. For the next five hundred years, the youth of Ireland and their disciples fanned out across Europe, winning converts, making disciples and multiplying missionary outposts. Wherever they went they carried their books and their love of learning. They revitalized European culture and possibly saved civilization following the fall of the Roman Empire.

## CHARACTERISTICS OF A MISSIONARY MOVEMENT

God takes the initiative. God chooses unlikely people, far from the center of ecclesiastical power, and he works to remake them from the inside out. He inspires innovative insights regarding his mission and how it is to be carried out. Biblical truths and practices are rediscovered. A growing band of ordinary people emerges who have a heartfelt faith and missionary zeal that knows no bounds. Despite opposition from powerful forces within society and the existing church, the gospel spreads into unreached fields. The existing church is renewed, and society is transformed.

Eventually every movement declines; it ceases to value the treasure stored in the world to come, and it begins to trust in the treasures it has found in this world. Meanwhile God goes looking for another lonely shepherd boy who is cold, hungry and a long way from home.

The life-cycle pattern of new life, growth, maturity and decline is a recurring theme of history. This book deals with the characteristics of missionary movements in their most dynamic expression. From Patrick's story we can identify five key characteristics of movements that change the world.

*White-hot faith.* Movements often begin with individuals like

Patrick whose lives have been unraveled and redirected by God's intervention. Their example inspires others, and the movement begins to spread, fueled by the energy of a white-hot faith. This story of a great missionary movement began with a teenage boy who was broken, lonely and defeated. He lost his home, his family and his position in society. He had lost everything, but he found the love of God in Christ and a call to preach the gospel.

Movements that change the world may eventually come to possess resources, learning and power, but they do not begin with these things. Missionary movements begin with men and women who encounter the living God and surrender in loving obedience to his call.

*Commitment to a cause.* Nothing was more important to Patrick and his followers than their faith in Christ and his cause. They expected a high degree of commitment from themselves and from one another. They attracted the youth of Ireland who gladly devoted their lives to the spread of the gospel. Their "otherworldly" faith paradoxically enabled them to be fearless and uncompromising agents of transformation in this world.

A movement emerges when people commit to a cause. People who change the world live in alignment with their deeply held beliefs. A movement ceases to exist when no one cares anymore.

*Contagious relationships.* Patrick did not just win isolated individuals. His strategy was to reach whole clans with the gospel. Patrick removed unnecessary barriers to the spread of the gospel and the growth of the movement. The Scriptures were supreme, yet the monks had a love for both classical literature and the pagan poets. His missionary movement was at home in the existing culture and yet radically distinct from it.

When movements spread rapidly, they do so through preexisting networks of relationships. Networks of relationships are the means by which a movement expands. They also provide the building blocks that give a movement its strength.

*Rapid mobilization.* Patrick grew leaders from the people he reached. His missionaries did the same. There was a constant supply of workers moving throughout and beyond Ireland for centuries. They won new converts and recruited fresh workers wherever they traveled. None of this was centrally planned, funded or controlled. There was the expectation that the same Spirit who had inspired Patrick would inspire others to follow his example. These workers were not known for their polished Latin or abstract theology. They were known for their missionary zeal and devotion to Christ.

Missionary movements spread through the efforts of ordinary people. The rapid spread of the gospel requires the efforts of non-professionals who are not dependent on external funding and are not strictly controlled. Converts immediately begin sharing their faith and making disciples. Key leaders model effective ministry; they recruit and deploy workers, then train them on the job.

*Adaptive methods.* Patrick structured the Celtic church for the spread of the gospel. The missionary order was at the head of church life. In contrast to the static, rigid and anchored nature of the Roman church, Celtic monasticism was supremely adaptable, flexible and transferable. While the heart of the gospel remained the same, Patrick communicated the gospel in ways that affirmed the best of Celtic culture, ensuring that the Irish could follow Christ without having to become Romans. The forms changed to fit the context and to serve the needs of an expanding movement while the unchanging gospel remained at the center of the movement.

The most effective movements are prepared to change everything about themselves except their core beliefs. Unencumbered by tradition, movements feel free to experiment with new forms and strategies. Movements pursue their mission with methods that are effective, flexible and reproducible, which outlast and even surpass the influence of the first generation of leaders.

Whenever and wherever we find dynamic missionary movements, we will find each of these characteristics in some form. Before we go on to look at each one in depth, we need first to understand what movements are and why they are important.

# Introduction

*Why Movements Matter*

**L**et me tell you why movements matter to me. I walked away from my faith in my late teens and early twenties. It didn't take long for my life to unravel. I wasn't happy with God, and I wasn't happy without him. I didn't think living as a Christian was possible. Then along came an Australian guy named Bill Hallam. He'd come to know Christ on the hippie trail between Amsterdam and Delhi through a ministry called Dilaram, founded by Floyd and Sally McClung.[1]

I was impressed with Bill. There were times when I wanted to throw him out of my house because of the hard things he had to say, but I knew he loved me, and I knew that Christ had changed his life. I hoped my life could change too.

I gave up running from God. Six months later I'd saved enough money to travel from Australia to Holland and join Dilaram. It was the late 1970s. I ended up in Amsterdam on the "Ark"—Dilaram's discipleship community, located on two large houseboats on a canal behind the central railway station.

There I learned how to experience the love of God in prayer and worship. I learned how to communicate the gospel to travelers from all over the world. I saw broken lives restored by the power of the Word and the Spirit in the context of a discipleship community.

There was Jean Claude, a deserter from the French Foreign Legion who had come to faith. I was there the day Interpol came to arrest him. I shared a room with two former members of the Irish Republican Army, both new Christians. One eventually turned himself in and went to prison. I remember Dave, a six-foot-five-inch Scotsman and "rage-aholic," waving a hammer in front of my face and threatening to kill me. There were people with backgrounds in homosexuality, prostitution, Eastern religions and drugs. Every year around forty of them came to faith and began the journey of discipleship.

I didn't know it at the time, but Dilaram was a movement. It began when God called the McClungs. Floyd was in India with Youth With A Mission when he passed a beggar on the street and realized the beggar was a young Westerner who had fallen on hard times. There were thousands of hippies on the road from London to Delhi. Many were searching for truth but instead got dysentery and hepatitis and became addicted to drugs.

Floyd and Sally set up the first Dilaram House in Kabul, Afghanistan. They took in ill and drug-dependent hippies, nursed them, talked to them about Jesus and saw many come to know him. Soon Dilaram Houses were established in London, Amsterdam, Kathmandu and Delhi. Many of the workers for these houses had come to faith through Dilaram.

I never forgot the lessons I learned through my time with Dilaram: I discovered the love of God, the call to discipleship, the power of the gospel to change lives, the work of the Holy Spirit, the importance of prayer and Christian community, and God's heart for the nations. These lessons became part of me and have guided me ever since. I also didn't mind meeting Michelle, the Australian girl I would eventually marry, in Amsterdam.

God uses missionary movements like Dilaram to remake people and to make history. That's why they are important to me.

What I would like to do is help you understand the dynamics of missionary movements by telling stories and reflecting on the lessons they can teach us. I'd like to help you get in touch with the dreams God has given you to make a difference in the lives of lost people living in a broken world. I believe God can use these stories from history, from our contemporaries and from around the world to encourage our hearts, strengthen our resolve and teach us about how he works through his people.

If you want to be a disciple of Jesus and if you want to make disciples, this book is for you.

## MOVEMENTS THAT CHANGE THE WORLD

Before we move on we should clarify what a movement is. In a general sense, movements are informal groupings of people and organizations pursuing a common cause. They are people with an agenda for change. Movements don't have members, but they do have participants. The goals of a movement can be furthered by organizations, but organizations are not the totality of a movement. A movement can have leading figures, but no one person or group controls a movement. Movements are made up of people committed to a common cause.

Think of the environmental movement. Where are its headquarters? Where is the organization or leader who controls this movement? The reality is that the environmental movement is composed of an array of interconnected leading figures, organizations and participants. They may not all agree on the precise nature of their goals and methods, but they share a common cause.

For good or for evil, movements make history. So much of history is the result of the clash of movements vying over their conflicting visions of how the world should be.

Religious, cultural and political movements shaped the twentieth century. Wars were waged over nationalism, communism and Islamic fundamentalism. The civil rights movement, feminism, environmentalism and the gay rights movement set the social agenda in their day. A well-kept secret is that Pentecostalism, broadly defined, was the largest and most expansive movement of the twentieth century.

Movements are characterized by discontent, vision and action. Discontent unfreezes people from their commitment to the way things are. Movements emerge when people feel something needs to change. If the vacuum created by discontent is filled with a vision of a different future and action to bring change, then a movement is born.

Movements change people, and changed people change the world.

## WHAT JESUS STARTED

Jesus was the first missionary. He didn't start an organization, he didn't write a book, and he didn't run for office. What Jesus did was to found a missionary movement that would one day span the globe.

Jesus began his life and ministry far from the center of power. He was a carpenter's son with a basic education. He was not formally trained as a rabbi. He was without social status and wealth. What mattered to Jesus was his relationship with his Father. He spent long hours in prayer. The Hebrew Scriptures permeated his life and his teaching. He won his victory over Satan by surrendering to the Father as an obedient Son.

Jesus went from town to town demonstrating the compassion and power of God as he healed the sick and cast out demons. He sought out people who were responsive to his message: fishermen, tax collectors, farmers, prostitutes, soldiers, beggars and notorious sinners. His mission was to seek and to save them by giving his life as a ransom for them.

Jesus bypassed the religious and community leaders, and called ordinary people to join his missionary band. He called them to be with him, and he promised to teach them how to catch people. He taught them as they traveled together by foot and by boat, as he ministered to thousands and as he ministered to individuals.

Jesus spoke to crowds in the open air. He told stories to groups over a meal. He talked to individuals alone. He communicated with power and with simplicity, trusting the Father for the outcome.

When Jesus' disciples had learned just enough to be dangerous, he sent them out with empty pockets to preach, heal the sick and cast out demons.

Jesus contended fearlessly with his opponents and never gave ground. He called his hearers to turn from their sin and to turn to God for mercy and forgiveness. He set his face to go to Jerusalem and die a shameful criminal's death. He entrusted his life and the fruit of his ministry to God.

God the Father raised Jesus from the dead, defeating sin and death and Satan. Just when Jesus' disciples thought the job was done and it was time to put their feet up, Jesus commanded them to go and make disciples of every nation. He did not offer them resources or a plan. He just commanded them to go and promised his presence through the Holy Spirit.

That's how the mission of Jesus became a missionary movement.

The church Jesus founded was a missionary church. Its existence and activities were an expression of its missionary calling.[2] Its members were fearlessly determined to win others to faith in Jesus as the crucified and risen Messiah. Their mission field began at home in Jerusalem and Judea, and it extended to the ends of the earth. The goal and purpose of their missionary work was the making of disciples and the creation of communities of disciples— people who turned from their old way of life, put their trust in Jesus and obeyed his teaching.[3]

There is no other foundation for our mission than the good news of Christ crucified for our sins. Paul says the message of the cross is offensive to sinful humanity. It was offensive to Paul until he met Jesus on the Damascus road. Our mission is to proclaim the good news about Jesus in words and deeds by the power of the Holy Spirit.

The New Testament is a missionary document.[4] The Gospels tell the story of what Jesus *began* to do and teach, and Acts is about what Jesus continued to do through the Holy Spirit (see Acts 1:1). In Acts people were converted and gathered into new churches. The New Testament epistles were written by missionaries concerned with the spiritual growth of Jesus' followers in community and in mission. If the early church had not been a missionary church—sharing the gospel of Jesus and making disciples—there would have been no church.

Our English words *mission, missionary* and *missional* come from the Latin *missio*, meaning "the act of sending." *Missio* is the equivalent of the New Testament Greek word *apostle* from *apostolos*, meaning "one who is sent." Jesus told his disciples, "As the Father has *sent* me, I am *sending* you." Then he breathed on them and said, "Receive the Holy Spirit" (John 20:21-22, italics mine). Alan Hirsch reminds us that "the mission of God flows directly through every believer and every community of faith that adheres to Jesus."[5] The church, in its very essence, is a missionary/missional movement with a mandate to carry on the ministry of Jesus in the power of the Spirit—to take the good news of Jesus to the world.

Today there appears to be some confusion over the terms *missionary* and *missional* when used as descriptors of the church. The words are identical in meaning. They refer to being sent by God into the world. Unfortunately, when we hear the word *missionary* we tend to think of crosscultural or overseas mission, whereas when we hear the word *missional* the focus tends to be on mission in a first-world, postmodern context. The mission of God knows no such cultural or geographic boundaries. There is only one missionary/missional mandate. There is only one missionary/missional church. There is only one missionary/missional movement that Jesus founded.

Mission has a threefold reality.[6] First, there is a message: mission assumes a distinct view of truth concerning the nature of God and the nature of salvation. Second, mission involves the communication of both truth and a new way of life. Third, the purpose of mission is conversion. People accept the message, are integrated into the community of faith and begin to practice a new way of life—a new life committed to following Jesus and sharing the truth about him with others.

As a missionary movement, our message centers on Jesus Christ, the Son of God, who was crucified for our sin and is the only source of salvation for a lost world.

Second, as a missionary movement we have an agenda for change. Jesus calls all who would follow him to a new life of obedience to his will.

Third, mission involves the conversion of individuals and their inclusion into the body of Christ, which is the church, the people of God. There is no mission without the church, and there is no discipleship without the community of faith.

If this is what it means to be the missionary people of God, what do "missionaries" do? Missiologist Eckhard Schnabel explains:

Missionaries establish contact with non-Christians, they proclaim the news of Jesus the Messiah and Savior (proclamation, preaching, teaching, instruction), they lead people to faith in Jesus Christ (conversion, baptism), and they integrate the new believers into the local community of the followers of Jesus (Lord's Supper, transformation of social and moral behavior, charity).[7]

We have the message of the cross. We have new life in Christ. We have a mandate to make disciples and multiply churches— everywhere. We are a missionary people.

## WHY WE'RE NOT ALL THE SAME

I was corrupted in my first year of theological college. I discovered that church history is not just the history of ideas and events; it is also the history of movements. The church through history has been in a constant state of upheaval and change, decline and resurgence.

Christianity is a movement of movements—monasticism, evangelicalism and Pentecostalism, to name a few. These movements can find expression in movement organizations such as mission agencies and denominations. Movements are one of the key means by which God brings renewal and expansion to the church in its mission.

Each new movement has a unique contribution to make to the kingdom—its "founding charism" or gift of grace.[8] Monasticism modeled a deep devotion to Christ in the face of growing nominalism in the church. The Franciscans' gift to the church and the world was God's heart for the poor. The Reformation upheld the authority of Scripture and restored the truth of salvation by grace through faith. The Anabaptists emphasized the importance of discipleship and the believers' church. The Moravians were an inspiration as the first Protestant missionary order. The Methodists and Salvation Army combined evangelistic zeal and holiness with a heart for the poor. The Pentecostals rediscovered the untamed power of the Holy Spirit.

Where would we be today without the influence of these movements? What would we be left with today if their contributions were erased from history? They all had their shortcomings, yet God was at work through them, renewing his church in faithfulness to Christ and his cause.

The great church historian Kenneth Scott Latourette argued

that one of the indications of the vitality of the Christian faith is the emergence of new movements. The periods of the greatest vigor and expansion of the Christian faith are the periods in which new movements arise.[9] The Christian movement is like a garden. A healthy garden is a diverse ecosystem; new plants are always coming into existence, other plants are flourishing, and still others are dying and decaying. The garden lives on in a continuing state of renewal. It is through the birth and growth of new movements of churches and mission entities that God has renewed the Christian movement down through the ages.

In the renewal and expansion of the church, the breakthroughs *always* occur on the fringe of ecclesiastical power—*never* at the center.[10] In every generation, in some obscure place, God is beginning something new. That's where we need to be.

### IS THIS BOOK FOR YOU?

If you're a follower of Jesus, you don't have to start a missionary movement. You're already in one. This book is about helping you to understand what this means and how to participate in what God is already doing.

When I wrote this book, I had some people in mind. I thought of Mark and Fiona, who have seen eighteen people come to know Christ over the last year and are wondering if these people are the beginning of a church plant.

I thought of Oscar, a pastor in Kenya who has grown a church from a dozen people to thousands. Even more important, the leaders he has grown are now planting churches in the suburbs and the slums of Nairobi, and that's just the beginning.

I thought of Pauline in China, a young woman in her twenties who is winning her friends to Christ and baptizing them secretly in a bathtub. She has a vision to multiply small house fellowships in her city.

I thought of Wayne and his team, who go visiting door to door in their impoverished community every week, caring for the sick, praying for people in need, helping out in practical ways and sharing the good news of Jesus. Wayne is wondering what it will take to reach this town and to send out teams into other towns.

I thought of Tim, the pastor of a large church in New York. He has a vision to see his city transformed by the gospel. Tim is growing leaders and sending them out to plant churches. He is partnering with anyone he can find who is willing to plant gospel-centered churches. He has a heart for the cities of the world.

I thought of Gary, who runs his own business and in his spare time has a ministry to high school students. Forty of them have come to know Christ. Gary can't understand why his local church leaders are not embracing this work of God. He wonders what he should do next.

I'm writing for people like these. They and others like them have also been my teachers. As I've listened to their stories and the stories of countless others down through the ages, they have become my cloud of witnesses to the God revealed in Jesus and his mission in the world.

There is no formula, and there are no ten simple steps. We are workers in *God's* harvest field. We are utterly dependent on God for our salvation and for the results of our ministries. Nothing can explain the spread of the Christian movement throughout history other than the power of God that is present in the communication of the gospel of the crucified and risen Jesus Christ.[11]

What follows are the stories and lessons of our contemporaries and of those who have gone before us. They planted and they watered, but it is God who gave the growth.

**1**

# White-Hot Faith

*About three in the morning as we were continuing instant in prayer, the power of God came mightily upon us, insomuch that many cried out for exceeding joy and many fell to the ground. As soon as we were recovered a little from that awe and amazement at the presence of his majesty we broke out with one voice, "We praise thee O God; we acknowledge thee to be the Lord."*

JOHN WESLEY

**A sixteen-year-old boy is taken** captive by raiders and sold into slavery. Desperate with loneliness, hunger and cold, he cries out for deliverance, and God answers. He goes on to pioneer one of the greatest missionary movements the world has ever seen.

An obscure Augustinian monk agonizes over what it means to be made right with God through faith. His intense struggle is the catalyst for the Protestant Reformation.

A young minister returns from the mission field, a failure in his own eyes and devoid of the experience of God's loving acceptance. His heart is "strangely warmed" by the grace of God, and one of the most significant awakenings in modern history shakes Britain and spreads worldwide.

Patrick of Ireland, Martin Luther and John Wesley—we remember them as powerful historical figures through whom God renewed the church and transformed the world. We honor them as heroes of the faith. We forget they began as broken men crying out to God for an encounter that would change their lives. Out of their personal encounters with God, these transformational leaders went on to renew the church and to shape the world in which we live.

For a number of years I have taught a church planting course for the Salvation Army in Sydney. I enjoy going back each year not only for the interaction with the students but also because of the location. The conference center sits on a hill above the northern beaches of Sydney overlooking the Pacific Ocean.

Sydney has the most expensive real estate in Australia, and every year one of the officers reminds me that the Salvation Army once owned the land for as far as the eye can see. In 1900, Miss Elizabeth Jenkins bequeathed hundreds of acres of farming land to the Salvation Army. Today that land would be worth hundreds of millions of dollars. The problem is that much of the land was carved up and sold off over the years for housing or was acquired by the state government for community use.

Every year I'm told, "Imagine what we could achieve if only we had that property today." The trap is set. We go back into the next session. Then I remind them that at one time the Salvation Army consisted of William and Catherine Booth sitting at their kitchen table, with no other resource than the call of God.

Church history is not made by well-financed, well-resourced individuals and institutions. History is made by men and women of faith who have met with the living God. Without faith it is impossible to please God.

I learned this lesson the hard way in our first church plant. Halfway through the second year, the church experienced intense conflict. I wondered how I would make it through. Since launching the new church, we had added a new family every week, and we were at over two hundred people. Naturally, as growth equals success, I thought I was the world's best church planter. Then a church fight erupted, and my world came crashing down. I wanted to fight or run, and God just told me to stand.

Soon after, I heard John Wimber of the Vineyard movement say, "Jesus wants his church back." I realized that was my issue. Jesus wanted his church back, and he wanted me back.

I began seeking God like never before. I would rise early and go out into my garage, stoke up a small wood heater, and pray and read the Scriptures. This was not discipline; it was desperation. One morning alone in the garage, I had a strong sense of God saying, "It's not about just one new church; it's about a whole new generation of churches." From that moment, my calling has been to fuel church planting movements across Australia and beyond.

It took a few more months before peace was restored in our church. A few people left. Most stayed. God's blessing returned, but I was never the same again.

Profound encounters with God are important catalysts in the formation of movements for the renewal and expansion of the Christian faith. Social and political factors influenced the Protestant Reformation, but religious convictions and experiences centered on Jesus were the chief catalysts for change.

Valid experiences of God will be in harmony with his Word and must find expression in action. A white-hot faith is concerned with the Spirit, the Word and the world. It aims to produce right-heartedness, right thinking and right action. It calls for the consecration of heart, head and hands.[1] Fresh encounters with God through the Word and the Spirit provide compelling authority that energizes a missionary movement to go and change the world.

## THE FIRST PROTESTANT MISSIONARY MOVEMENT

*I have only one passion, 'tis He, 'tis only He.*

COUNT NIKOLAUS VON ZINZENDORF

At the end of the seventeenth century, Protestantism in Europe was entering a religious ice age, frozen by passionless orthodoxy. Since the death of Martin Luther, 150 years had passed, and still no significant missionary movement had emerged from the Reformation.

For centuries the religious orders—the Benedictines, Carmelites, Augustinians, Franciscans and Dominicans—had been the wellspring of life for the renewal and expansion of the Catholic faith. In the regions they controlled, the Reformers abolished these orders without creating a functional equivalent. Protestantism was bereft of a mechanism for world missions until two young Moravians, one a potter and the other a carpenter, decided it was time to act.

When Leonard Dober and David Nitschmann set out to take the gospel to the West Indies in 1732, William Carey, the "father of Protestant missions," had not yet been born. Hudson Taylor, missionary pioneer, would not arrive in China for another 150 years. Dober and Nitschmann were the first missionaries sent out by the Moravian Brethren; within twenty years Moravian missionaries were in the Arctic among the Eskimos, in southern Africa, among the Indians of North America, and in Suriname, Ceylon, China, India and Persia.

The Moravian Brethren originated in the Czech regions of Moravia and Bohemia in central Europe. They traced their roots back to the Czech reformer Jan Hus, who had been condemned as a heretic, excommunicated and burned at the stake by the Roman Catholic Church in 1415. Hus inspired the birth of the first Protestant church to break with Rome, one hundred years before Martin Luther.

When the Reformation came, the Moravians forged links with the Reformers, including Luther and Calvin. In the 1620s the

Moravians lost the protection of the local nobility and suffered severe persecution by the Catholic Church. Their churches were closed, and they were hunted down and imprisoned. Some were tortured and executed, while others were forced into hiding or fled into exile. For the next one hundred years, the Moravian Brethren barely survived as an underground church—hardly the sort of people you would expect to launch a missionary movement.

The plight of the Moravians caught the attention of a young Austrian noble, Count Nikolaus von Zinzendorf. As a young boy, Zinzendorf had devoted his life to Christ and the spread of the gospel throughout the world. In 1722 he opened his estate in Saxony as a sanctuary for the persecuted Moravians. With his help they built a village and called it Herrnhut, which meant "the Lord's watch." Zinzendorf set up a number of projects to serve this community, including a bookshop, a dispensary, a school and a printing press for cheap editions of the Bible and other literature.

By 1727 a steady stream of religious refugees had arrived—some with Lutheran, Reformed, Anabaptist and even Catholic backgrounds. Each had a dream for the church restored; reality, however, proved to be quite different. It was hard for men and women who had suffered for their convictions to sacrifice those convictions for the sake of harmony. Factions developed, and this led to bitter disputes and broken relationships.

Zinzendorf was under pressure from local authorities to shut down this "hotbed of heresy." He could have relied on his power as a feudal lord to expel the warring factions. Instead, Zinzendorf stepped in to restore peace. He and his family moved out of their mansion into the village. He devoted all his time, energy and wealth to serving the people. He spent long hours and days meeting with individuals and groups to restore harmony. He opened the Scriptures and helped the community to understand the mind of God.

Zinzendorf introduced structure into the community. He appointed leaders on the basis of character and spiritual maturity. He drew up a set of forty-two statutes as the basis for community life and divided the whole community into "bands." Each band consisted of two or three people of the same gender who met to open their hearts and to encourage, correct and pray for one another. People were reconciled as they confessed their sins and made renewed commitments to live together in love. Night and day, Herrnhut became a center for prayer and worship.

By the summer of 1727 there was a "contagious and holy expectancy" at Herrnhut. Something wonderful was about to happen. On August 13 the Moravians experienced what can only be described as a Pentecostal outpouring of the Holy Spirit. As they celebrated the Lord's Supper the Spirit moved among them; their hearts were set on fire with new faith and love toward the Savior and with burning love toward one another. They embraced each other in tears. God breathed new life into their centuries-old movement.

Manifestations of the Holy Spirit's power continued, including divine healing. People met in small bands to confess their sins and pray for one another that they might be healed. The factions dissolved. Night watches and prayer vigils were established. Prayer was offered up around the clock, seven days a week, and continued uninterrupted for the next one hundred years.

This spiritual renewal was channeled into mission. Four years later Zinzendorf was visiting the court of the king of Denmark where he met Anthony Ulrich, an African slave from the West Indies. Ulrich had come to faith in Christ and met two Moravians at court. He poured out his heart to Zinzendorf as he described the shameful conditions of the slaves on the Danish island of St. Thomas. He spoke of his sister and brother and of their desire to hear the gospel. Zinzendorf was deeply moved and excited by the missionary challenge.

It was the following year when Leonard Dober, the potter, and David Nitschmann, the carpenter, became the first Moravian missionaries. Zinzendorf spent the whole night before they left in prayer. He rose early and drove them in his carriage as far as he could. Before parting, they knelt by the roadside to receive his blessing. They carried their bundles on their backs as they walked away with just thirty shillings in their pockets. Zinzendorf had no other instructions to give them than "to do all in the Spirit of Jesus Christ."

Dober and Nitschmann had little understanding of what life would be like in the West Indies. They had no mission agency to support them. They had no example to follow. As they walked toward the port, they had no idea that they were clearing the way for the birth of the Protestant missionary movement.

These two young men became the founders of the Christian movement among the slaves of the West Indies. By the time other Christian missionaries arrived, fifty years later, the Moravians had baptized 13,000 converts and planted churches on the islands of St. Thomas, St. Croix, Jamaica, Antigua, Barbados and St. Kitts.

The Moravians were the first Protestants to treat world missions as the responsibility of the whole church.[2] Under Zinzendorf, the Moravians became an intense and highly mobile missionary movement. Within two decades the Moravians sent out more missionaries than all Protestants had sent out in the previous two hundred years. The rapid deployment of so many young missionaries around the world was remarkable.

The outreach was made possible by a relative lack of concern with training, finances or structure.[3] All of these missionaries were laypeople, mostly peasant farmers and tradesmen. They were trained as evangelists, not academic theologians. They received enough money to get to the port. The missionaries then worked for their passage across the ocean. On the mission field, they took up whatever work would provide enough food and clothing. They had no formal theological education, and they received scant training in language acquisition and crosscultural ministry. Once they set sail, they had no financial support and no organization to look after them; there was no guarantee of health care, only the likelihood that they would never see their homeland again.

Over the next 150 years, 2,158 Moravians volunteered to serve overseas in the most remote, unfavorable and neglected areas. This was something new in the expansion of Christianity: an entire Christian community—families as well as singles—devoted to world missions.[4]

The impact of the Moravians did not end with their own achievements. They profoundly influenced both William Carey, known as the "father of Protestant missions," and John Wesley, the founder of the Methodist movement. The Moravians prepared the way for the great Protestant missionary expansion of the nineteenth century.

Zinzendorf did not want to set up an independent Moravian church. His aim was to promote the unity of all Christians. Zinzendorf saw the Moravian movement as a missionary community—a church within the church—and all Moravians as "soldiers of the Lamb."[5] Christianity began the nineteenth century as a predominately European faith bound by traditionalism. By the end of the nineteenth century, Christianity was well on the way to becoming a truly global movement.

Zinzendorf described the members of the Moravian movement as "the Savior's happy people." The rallying cry of the Moravian missionary movement was: "May the Lamb that was slain receive the reward of his sufferings." Only the Moravians' supreme happiness in the Lamb can explain the freedom they had to sacrifice everything to carry the power and the fellowship of the crucified Christ across the world.[6]

## WHEN THE SPIRIT COMES WITH POWER

*The kingdom of heaven belongs to the violent who lay hold upon it. But this violence is not accepted by God unless the person practicing it is*

*ready himself to bear the shock in return. Whoever wrestles with God in*
*prayer puts his whole life at stake.*

JACQUES ELLUL

In the history of the church it has been spiritual experiences that have given birth to movements of renewal and expansion.

April 9, 2006, marked one hundred years since the Azusa Street revival catapulted Pentecostalism onto the world stage. William Seymour, the thirty-four-year-old son of former slaves, led this revival. Early Pentecostalism emphasized the "baptism of the Holy Spirit," evidenced by speaking in tongues and the restoration of the true church before Jesus returns. The emotionally charged meetings ran all day and into the night. There was no central coordination of the meetings, and Seymour rarely preached. He taught the people to cry out to God for sanctification, the baptism with the Holy Spirit and divine healing.[7]

Immediately, missionaries fanned out from Azusa Street to the world. Within two years they had brought Pentecostalism to parts of Asia, South America, the Middle East and Africa. They were poor, untrained and unprepared. Many died on the field. Nevertheless, their sacrifices were rewarded; the Pentecostal/charismatic movement became the fastest growing and most globally diverse expression of worldwide Christianity. Some researchers predict that, at the current rate of growth, there will be one billion Pentecostals by 2025, most of them in Asia, Africa and Latin America.[8]

Pentecostalism is perhaps the fastest expanding movement— religious, cultural or political—ever. Communism, fascism and militant Islam shaped the last century, but none of them matched the impact of Pentecostalism. Pentecostals are often identified with the high-profile individuals who appear on religious television in the United States. The reality, however, is that the vast majority of Pentecostals live in the global South, or the developing world. The regions of Africa, Asia and South America where Pentecostalism is growing the fastest also have the world's youngest and fastest-growing populations. If there is a "typical" Pentecostal, it is a poor woman living in a Nigerian village or a Brazilian shantytown.[9] Such people are the new face of Christianity, and they are also its future.

Pentecostal faith has a very down-to-earth influence in the developing world. An increasing volume of sociological research from Venezuela, to Jamaica, to Ghana, is showing how evangelical Christianity is remaking the lives of the poor—spiritually, morally and materially. Pentecostalism in particular is proving more potent than government programs and social movements in improving the lives of the poor and marginalized.[10]

Pentecostalism reminds us that to change the world, we must first be changed. Religious zeal launched its staggering global expansion, so that what began as a revival meeting has become a global missionary movement. There are two means by which God develops such white-hot faith in us: *crisis* and *process*. In the moment of *crisis*, we learn to surrender to the grace of God. The practice of spiritual disciplines is the *process* that deepens our life in God.

## CRISIS: A SURRENDERED LIFE

The truck arrived at the house we were renovating. The concrete pour was on. We had just twenty minutes to empty the truck of its load. After that time the driver would expect payment for every minute he waited. Three carpenters and their laborer dropped their tools, and each grabbed a wheelbarrow. I was the laborer.

The pace was frantic. Wheelbarrows were lined up waiting to be filled. Wet concrete is heavy and unstable. I took off down the driveway with a full load. I ran around the side of the house, through the mud to the back where we were laying the foundations for an extension. I braced myself for the last challenge—getting my wheelbarrow down a slippery plank and under the house to drop my load.

Just as I was about to take the plunge, I heard the booming voice of the foreman: "Watch out! We don't have a good laborer here."

Choking back the emotions, I made it down the plank, emptied the wheelbarrow and headed back up around the house to pick up my next load. I felt totally beaten. "We don't have a good laborer here." The church plant wasn't coming together like I'd hoped. Personally, we had a couple of financial crises every week. We had two young children and one on the way. The strain was showing in our marriage, and I was barely holding it together. But I was right in the center of God's will and purpose. I had nowhere to run.

By the time I made it back up to the truck, I had determined in my heart there was no going back. I would stay the course. I would surrender my life and future to God and trust him with the outcome of my ministry.

This was to be the first of half a dozen opportunities over the next eighteen months to come to the place of surrender. I thought once would be enough. God had other plans.

Throughout the Scriptures, when God takes the initiative to call a person to his service, it is often through a powerful encounter. Jesus' baptism and wilderness experience; the transformation of the disciples at Pentecost; and Paul's encounter with Christ on the Damascus road—these were all "crisis" experiences. God intervenes in the midst of desolation and seeks a response.

This pattern continues throughout the history of the Christian movement. Deep experiences of surrender precede revelation of God's purposes and the outpouring of power to achieve his will. At the point of surrender, we renounce dependence on anything but the presence and power of God. All we bring is our brokenness and our need. It is God who initiates, and it is God's grace that transforms.

Experiences of crisis, surrender and empowerment are scattered throughout the stories of every missionary movement. They touch the lives of founders and empower ordinary people to do extraordinary things. As people learn to go to the cross and find God there, they witness the power of the resurrection and the coming of the Holy Spirit. Those realities are the foundation out of which they minister.

## PROCESS: A DISCIPLINED LIFE

The other dimension of cultivating a white-hot faith is *process*— the disciplined life. Spiritual disciplines may vary from movement to movement, but they are all activities that deepen our relationship with God.

Every dynamic movement finds its unique mix of spiritual disciplines. The early followers of Christ met regularly to read the Scriptures and hear the teaching of the apostles. They met for prayer and to share the Lord's Supper; they also confessed their sins to one another. Spiritual disciplines were integrated into the rhythm of their lives. The monastic movement practiced *lectio divina*, or prayerful reflection on the Scriptures. At the heart of the Jesuit order were the *Spiritual Exercises of Ignatius Loyola,* thirty days of prayerful meditation on the life, ministry and death of Jesus. The Moravians and Methodists had classes and bands— accountability groups for prayer and the confession of sin. Members of the Student Volunteer Movement valued "the morning watch"—a daily time of Bible study and devotional prayer. Evangelicals are known for their expositional preaching and teaching of the Scriptures. Pentecostals place high value on experiencing God in corporate worship.

No movement can be sustained on crisis experiences alone. Spiritual disciplines prepare the way for, and support, life-changing experiences. All the great movement pioneers learned both to surrender to God in crisis *and* to seek his grace through the practice of spiritual disciplines. Their secret is the joy they experience as they discover that Christ is sufficient. Such men and women, of whom the world is not worthy (Heb 11:38), have conquered nations, fed the poor, crossed oceans, climbed mountain ranges, and endured persecution, imprisonment and death—all for the sake of the gospel. Their fellowship is with Jesus in his sufferings and in his joy. They display white-hot faith.

## JESUS AND WHITE-HOT FAITH

*When they saw the courage of Peter and John and realized that they were unschooled, ordinary men, they were astonished and they took note that these men had been with Jesus.*

ACTS 4:13

At the birth of the Christian movement, we don't find its founder in the temple at Jerusalem impressing the scholars with his learning and piety. We don't find him at the head of crowds of supporters who are impressed with his power to heal the sick and cast out demons. He's not wooing kings and governors. At the birth of the Christian movement Jesus is alone in the wilderness—hungry, thirsty and weary from a battle with Satan.

Jesus, the obedient Son, was waiting in the presence of his Father. Humble, dependent, broken, needy—every support had been taken away. Every consolation had gone. There was only the cost of obedience and abandonment and the horrifying prospect of the cross. Each temptation was an attack on his Sonship. Each temptation sought to have Jesus prove his identity through miraculous power rather than dependence, obedience and suffering. Jesus prevailed and returned victorious over evil, but the battle with Satan continued throughout his public ministry until the final defeat of evil on the cross.

It was in the place of desolation that Jesus' identity and call were tested. He refused to take charge of his destiny, choosing instead the path of obedience and triumphing over the tempter, thus leading the way for all who would follow. Here is the founda-

tion stone of the Christian movement: the heart of Jesus surrendered to the Father. Jesus was satisfied in the Father's love and
purpose. All else was forsaken.

Jesus repeatedly withdrew to be alone with the Father in
prayer—early in the morning, up on the mountainside, in the desert and sometimes for a whole night. He prayed when he was under
great strain. He prayed when he had important decisions to make.
He prayed as he faced the prospect of crucifixion. He prayed on
the cross itself.

The love of God was so real to Jesus, so compelling, that when
he turned to God in prayer, the cry that naturally came to his lips
was *Abba*, the Aramaic word for father. No other Jew had ever
spoken of God as Abba, but Jesus always addressed God in this
way, and he taught his disciples to do the same.[11]

Jesus taught his followers to expect the same intimacy with the
Father and the same power to be witnesses to the ends of the
earth. Before they could experience the power of God, they had to
face their utter dependence on him. When Jesus called Simon, Andrew, James and John, they were in a position of helplessness.
They had fished all night and caught nothing. At the command of
Jesus, they let down their nets one more time and hauled in a miraculous catch. As a result, Peter was overwhelmed by the presence of God in Jesus. He fell at Jesus' feet and confessed his un-
worthiness and his sin. He left his fishing boat and his business
partners and followed Jesus immediately and unconditionally. His
reaction reminds us of the Old Testament prophets who received
their calls as they were overwhelmed in the presence of God.[12]

The religious leaders saw the boldness of the early disciples,
and they were amazed, for Peter and John were "unschooled, ordinary men." What set Peter and John apart? They had been with
Jesus (Acts 4:13). The disciples' transformation from a scattered
band of defeated and despairing men into the leaders of a dynamic
missionary movement was achieved through their shared experi-

ence of the risen Son and his Holy Spirit. The expansion of early Christianity was more than a social phenomenon or human enterprise. It was the Lord himself who "added" believers to the church when the gospel was preached (Acts 2:47).

The apostle Paul was a well-educated, intelligent and determined man. He boasted of his religious pedigree and accomplishments, but these attributes were nothing to him compared to the power of knowing Christ. His encounter on the Damascus road was all about relinquishing his abilities and credentials and surrendering to the risen Christ. Paul told the Corinthians that the troubles he experienced had pushed him beyond his ability to endure. Yet in the midst of despair he experienced the comfort of God and the power of God (2 Cor 1:3-11). Paul's troubles taught him that the treasure of the gospel is carried in fragile jars of clay; this truth emphasized that the gospel's power comes from God alone, not from the messenger (2 Cor 4:7-12).

You can run an institution with systems of command and control, but Jesus founded a movement, not an institution. He brought his followers into the same experience he had with God the Father and God the Holy Spirit; then he sent them to the ends of the earth with nothing but the message of salvation and the reality of God's power. A passionate faith is at the heart of every dynamic missionary movement. It is the greatest resource. Today, where Christianity is expanding rapidly in the developing world, it is often the only resource.

## CHRISTIANITY GOES SOUTH

*As I travel, I have observed a pattern, a strange historical phenomenon of God "moving" geographically from the Middle East, to Europe to North America to the developing world. My theory is this: God goes where he is wanted.*

PHILIP YANCEY

For the last five hundred years the story of Christianity has been bound up with Europe and European-derived cultures. Historian Philip Jenkins records how since the beginning of the twentieth century the center of gravity in the Christian world has shifted southward to Africa, Asia and Latin America.[13] These are the regions in which the largest and fastest-growing Christian communities on the planet are found. They are also the regions of fastest population growth. If these trends continue, by 2050, only about one-fifth of the world's three billion Christians will be non-Hispanic whites. While Northern Hemisphere Christianity is in decline, a new era of Southern Christianity has dawned.

In 1900, colonial Africa had a population of 108 million people, of whom 8.7 million, or 9 percent, were Christian. The majority of those Christians were Coptic and Ethiopian Orthodox. They were outnumbered by 34.5 million Muslims—a ratio of 4:1. By 1962, after Africa had shaken off colonial rule, there were about 145 million Muslims and 60 million Christians—a ratio of about 5:2. By 1985 a major expansion of the Christian faith had taken place in the midst of the pessimism and turmoil of post-independent Africa. The churches were often the only viable structures remaining after the breakdown of state institutions. Ironically, Christian African converts came predominantly from the poor and marginalized. There were over 16,500 conversions a day and an annual growth of six million people.[14]

By 2000 there were 360 million Christians in Africa. David Barrett estimated that in the year 2000, 40.6 percent of Africans were Muslim and 45 percent were Christian. From 1900 to 2000 the ratio of Muslims to Christians shifted from 4:1 to less than 1:1. If current trends continue, by 2025, there could be 633 million Christians in Africa, making it the second largest Christian continent after South America (see table 1 on page 52).

Southern Christians, whether they are Catholic, evangelical or Pentecostal, are far more conservative in beliefs and in moral teaching than the Christians in the prosperous North. Christians

**Table 1. African Muslims and Christians (millions).** David B. Barrett, George T. Kurian and Todd M. Johnson, *World Christian Encyclopedia: A Comparative Survey of Churches and Religions in the Modern World*, 2nd ed. (New York: Oxford University Press, 2001), pp. 13-18; and Lamin Sanneh, *Whose Religion Is Christianity? The Gospel Beyond the West* (Grand Rapids: Eerdmans, 2003), pp. 14-15.

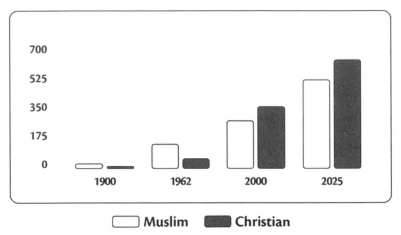

☐ Muslim  ■ Christian

of the global South have a supernatural view of the world and are more interested in personal salvation than in radical politics. They take the Bible seriously. They are more likely to believe that what they read in the Gospels is happening in their midst. They believe that the world of the apostles is a present reality. Jenkins observed, "If there is a single area of faith and practice that divides Northern and Southern Christians, it is the matter of spiritual forces and their effects on the everyday human world."[15]

Two years ago I was working hard at home on an article about the incredible spread of the Christian faith in the developing world when someone rang the doorbell. I was a little annoyed at the interruption, but reluctantly I opened the door. Two Chinese people wanted to tell me about Jesus. As we talked I discovered they were missionaries to Australia from Communist China. Eventually I returned to my writing with a living reminder that a new era has dawned in world missions. Fifty years ago the fledgling church in

China was reeling from the expulsion of Western missionaries and from persecution following the Communist takeover. Now fervent Chinese Christians are on my doorstep. Today the Chinese, Koreans, Indians, Brazilians, Nigerians and many others are the rising force in world missions.

British author Martin Robinson talks about some of the church planters from the developing world he has met in the West.[16] They come from Haiti, Brazil, Ethiopia, Colombia, Mexico, Nigeria and the Dominican Republic, to name a few. They often work, send money home to their extended families and plant a church at the same time. They are mechanics, cab drivers and laborers. Their hard work, faith, commitment and exuberance are infectious.

The center of gravity for the Christian faith has moved south. Again, renewal and expansion has come from the fringes.

God chooses what appears to be weak and foolish to shame what appears to be powerful and wise (1 Cor 1:27). Faith moves mountains.

**Trajectory of the Statistical Center of Global Christianity, A.D. 33-2100**
Todd M. Johnson and Sun Young Chung, "Tracking Global Christianity's Statistical Center of Gravity, A.D. 33–A.D. 2100," *International Review of Mission* 93 (April 2004): 166-81. Used by permission.

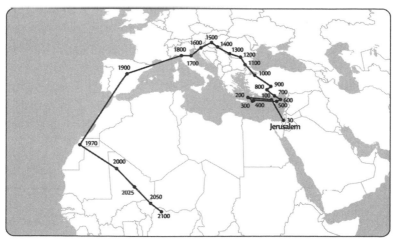

**CONCLUSION**

White-hot faith is the fuel that missionary movements run on.
Nothing happens without a deep dependence on God. Nothing
leads us into a healthy dependence on the power of God more
than to come face to face with our desperate need of him. Jesus is
the apostle and pioneer of our faith. He led the way for us in surrender to the will of God and the power of the Holy Spirit.

White-hot faith is an important factor whenever we see great
advances in the spread of the Christian faith. The stories of the
Moravians and the Pentecostals illustrate its impact. The great
movements of the Christian faith are only unleashed through the
presence and power of God in the midst of his people who are
faithful to his Word, led by his Spirit and engaged in his mission.
It is his harvest field. We are not passive bystanders but active
participants in what God is doing. We plant and we water, but
God gives the growth.

**2**

# Commitment to a Cause

*While women weep as they do now, I'll fight.*
*While little children go hungry as they do now, I'll fight.*
*While men go to prison in and out, in and out, I'll fight.*
*While there yet remains one dark soul without the light of God, I'll fight.*
*I'll fight to the very end.*

WILLIAM BOOTH, FOUNDER OF THE SALVATION ARMY

**In September 1980,** a thirty-seven-year-old electrician named Lech Walesa climbed over the barbed wire fences of the Lenin Shipyards in Gdansk, Poland, to join his comrades in their opposition to the communist oppression of the Soviet Union. Ten years later, Walesa was elected president of Poland; in nearby Soviet-controlled East Germany, as border guards looked on, the Berlin Wall was crumbling under the onslaught of demonstrators. The grip of communism on the Soviet Union and its satellite states had been broken; the Marxist dream of a communist utopia was no longer credible even to party members. A more compelling vision of a society built on individual freedom won the day.

It was not superior military might that defeated the communist empire. The authorities could have imprisoned and executed their opponents, as they had done in the past. They still had the power to unleash a nuclear nightmare. Communism dissolved as quickly as it had once emerged, but this second revolution took place with hardly a shot fired—an example of Victor Hugo's observation that "there is one thing stronger than all the armies in the world, and that is an idea whose time has come."[1]

Movements that change the world deal with the ultimate issues. They are causes that make demands on followers. Apathy changes nothing and is the surest sign that a movement, organization or society is in decline. Change takes place because people care enough to act on their deeply held beliefs. They choose "to live divided no more."[2]

Power does not finally depend on military or economic might but upon the ability to mobilize people around a cause.[3] Surprisingly, an eighteenth-century Anglican clergyman provides a very good example of this principle.

### THE METHODIST REVOLUTION

In 1737 a defeated and depressed Anglican missionary to the American colonies returned home to England. He despaired, saying, "I went to America, to convert the Indians; but oh! who shall convert me?"[4] The name of the missionary was John Wesley; he would go on to found the Methodist movement.

Through his contact with Moravian missionaries, Wesley saw the inadequacy of his own faith. He did not have the Moravians' joy and freedom in following Christ. He did not know the grace of God. In his journal entry of May 24, 1738, he described how he went unwillingly to a Moravian gathering at Aldersgate Street in London where they were studying the book of Romans. It was a quarter to nine, and as the leader was describing the change that God works in the heart through faith in Christ, Wesley felt his heart "strangely warmed." He wrote, "I felt I did trust in Christ alone for salvation; and an assurance was given me that He had taken away my sins, even mine, and saved me from the law of sin and death."[5]

What Wesley had sought to achieve in his own strength—assurance of salvation and power for living—he now received through dependence on God. The change in John Wesley unleashed one of the greatest movements in the history of the church.

Fired by his encounter with God at Aldersgate, Wesley traveled Britain with a vision to convert and disciple the nation and to renew the languishing church. In his own words, his mission was "to reform the nation, by spreading scriptural holiness over the land."[6] His goal was to establish a movement of people who were learning to obey Christ and to walk as he did.

Soon Wesley was preaching to huge crowds. Wesley's intensity of commitment led to conflict with the Church of England. He preached in church buildings when local clergy gave their permission, but often he was forced to follow the example of his friend George Whitefield and take the gospel to the open air. When Wesley was forbidden to speak in his father's former parish church, he stood outside on his father's tombstone and preached to thousands. In response to the clergy who had refused him access to the parishes they served, he declared, "The world is my parish!"

Wesley was not interested in just attracting crowds. What set Wesley apart was not the gospel he preached but his ability to gather converts into a disciplined movement. He wrote in his journal: "The devil himself desires nothing more than this, that the people of any place should be half-awakened and then left to themselves to fall asleep again. Therefore, I determine by the grace of God not to strike one stroke in any place where I cannot follow the blow."[7] As a brilliant strategist and innovator, he created and adapted structures that strengthened and united his followers, while facilitating the movement's rapid expansion.

Wesley multiplied a variety of groups—classes, bands and societies—to bring individuals to conversion and then to ensure their progress in discipleship. The requirement for joining a Methodist class was "a desire to flee from the wrath to come." Most conversions actually took place in the classes rather than through the field preaching. The classes were also the disciplinary unit of the movement. Inquiry was made into the state of each member's soul, and unrepentant offenders were removed from the fellowship. Howard Snyder describes the classes as "house churches" meeting in the various neighborhoods where people lived. The class leaders (both men and women) were pastors and disciplers.[8]

All Methodists were class members. Those who were clearly converted moved on to join the "bands." While the major focus of the class was on conversion and discipline, the focus of the band was confession and pastoral care. The "societies" were composed of all class and band members within a local area.

Wesley refused to preach Christian doctrine without discipline. He believed there could be no true Christianity without both; it was in fact better to lose members than to lose discipline. Methodism was a place to find support and accountability in the struggle against sin. A Methodist could not give up the fight and remain in the movement for very long. In 1748 Wesley visited the Bristol Methodist society and expelled 170 of its 900 members for reasons that included smuggling, cursing, drunkenness, wife beating and quarreling.[9] He wrote that to preach like an apostle without joining converts together to learn the ways of God "is only begetting children for the murderer."[10]

Wesley's words and actions may sound harsh to our ears; they help us understand why he polarized people in his own day. Today his commitment to holiness would have had him branded as a dangerous fundamentalist—which is probably why movement leaders are only "sainted" *after* they have died. But Wesley never used his power over the Methodist movement for personal gain. His strict discipline came from a deeply held conviction regarding the seriousness of sin and the imminent judgment of God. He really believed that people were lost without Christ. He really believed that sin brought destruction in this life and the next. He also believed that faith in Christ could, and should, result in loving obedience to Christ's commands.

Through Wesley's system of classes, bands and societies, Methodists united to encourage each other, confess their sins, pray for each other and hold one another accountable for their progress in the faith. Without this system for the care and mobilization of Methodist converts, Wesley would have only been known as a great evangelist, second to Whitefield. Instead he founded a movement that far exceeded his own personal achievements. He reached masses of people who were outside of the Anglican church, and turned thousands of them into workers committed to the cause of Methodism—traveling preachers, group leaders, educators, and visitors of the sick and of prisoners.

Every Methodist was expected to have a ministry. At least one in ten had a formal leadership position in the movement. Many of those leaders were women, including some of Wesley's preachers. Opponents among the Anglican clergy condemned this "prostituting of the ministerial function" and mocked the poor and illiterate Methodists who "pretended to be pregnant with a message from the Lord."[11] To Wesley, however, they were ministers of the gospel. He took an intense interest in their development, examining leaders and preachers every year to ensure their commitment, their character, their faith and their effectiveness. Methodists were issued "tickets of membership" that were renewed quarterly. Discipline and accountability at every level became a key distinctive of the Methodist movement.

Wesley was able to inspire commitment to the Methodist cause because he embodied that commitment. He endured opposition and derision from his peers in the church and in society. He defied the violence of the mobs that turned up to disrupt his meetings.

He lived an austere lifestyle and shunned every distraction to his calling. He endured the strain of constant travel on horseback and of long, hard days of work. He traveled almost a quarter of a million miles on horseback, preached 40,000 sermons and saw over 100,000 conversions. By the end of his life there were 71,463 Methodists in Britain and 61,811 in the United States.[12] Methodism was well on the way to becoming a worldwide movement. Today there are over 33 million Methodists worldwide and many more in the movements that Wesley inspired.

Although there were many factors that fed into this amazing expansion, none were more important than Methodists' discipline and commitment to their cause. Commitment to the cause is the currency that movements trade in. It's the air they breathe, the reason they exist.

## CULTIVATING COMMITMENT

Dynamic religious movements are clear about what they believe and why they exist. They don't confuse their beliefs with the beliefs of other faiths. They only admit and retain members who are fully committed to the beliefs and practices of the movement. They build strong ties between members for mutual support and accountability.

Like most movements, Methodism eventually drifted from high levels of commitment to leniency. It became an accepted institution of society and lost its evangelistic zeal. Practices such as the confession of sin in accountability groups faded away as its members became more refined and its clergy professionalized. Once commitment wanes, it is almost impossible to recover.[13]

Three factors enable a movement to maintain a strong commitment to its cause: founding charism, alignment and medium tension.

*Founding charism: Unique identity and calling.* To survive, every living thing is both constantly changing and constantly remaining the same. If an organism doesn't do both, it ceases to exist. Living organisms are constantly seeking self-renewal by referring back to their essential identity and adapting to their environment.[14] Likewise, movements must adapt to their changing environment while remaining true to their identity. (We will return to this topic when we look at "adaptive methods" in chapter five.)

The Catholic religious orders refer to their unique identity and mission as their "founding charism"—their founding gift of grace.[15] The most effective religious orders know who they are; they safeguard their founding charism over time even while they adapt to a changing world. Their methods may change, but the cause never does.

A clear identity and an agenda for change create a tension between the ideal promoted by a movement and its current reality. Transformational change is the outcome of that tension. Wesley's cause, for example, was the conversion and discipling of a nation, the renewal of a fallen church, and "scriptural holiness" spread throughout the land. He built everything around this central purpose and adapted structures and strategies to serve it. The result was an expanding movement that now spans several centuries.

Over time every movement wanders from its founding charism and can only be renewed by returning to it in a fresh way. That return must be both true to the movement's unique calling and innovative in how that calling is lived out.[16]

*Alignment: The mechanisms of commitment.* Having a clear identity and mission is only the beginning. Every aspect of the movement must be aligned with its overriding purpose. Wesley's system of classes, bands and societies ensured that he not only made converts but also channeled them into a disciplined and focused movement. His discipline of wayward members and regular examination of local leaders and circuit riders ensured commitment was maintained.

Effective movements develop "commitment mechanisms" that

ensure corporate and individual behavior is aligned with identity and purpose.[17] Commitment mechanisms include strong relational ties, personal sacrifice and the expectation of obedience to the norms of the group.

Researchers Jim Collins and Jerry Porras discovered that the truly great companies fostered a commitment to an ideology that was pervasive throughout the organization. For these companies, alignment was built into the selection and training of new staff, the screening out of staff who did not fit with the ideology and the promotion of those who did. These companies also actively promoted strong social bonds within the organization. They found alignment around a clear ideology enabled the best companies to turn their people loose to experiment, change, adapt and—above all—act.[18]

This is precisely what Wesley achieved. The Methodist cause was clear and reinforced by every aspect of Methodist life. Only those who remained committed to the cause remained within the movement. They poured their lives, their creativity, their time and their money into a cause they deeply believed in. This context of commitment empowered the Methodists to take the gospel to the ends of the earth.

*Medium tension: Distinct but connected.* Commitment to a cause attracts both admiration *and* opposition. Methodism, for example, attracted its fair share of ridicule from genteel society and violence from the mobs.

Such confrontation strengthens the resolve and unity of members within a movement, but there are limits to how high levels of commitment can become before they isolate a movement from the surrounding culture. Successful movements find the "medium tension" point with the surrounding environment.[19] Commitment levels are high, but not so high that potential members view joining the movement as a total break with their relationships and culture.

It is possible for a religious faith to be so alien to its surrounding culture as to make conversion highly unlikely, except for a limited number of social outsiders and misfits. If a movement is regarded as too deviant from the mainstream, it may only recruit those who are relationally isolated. However, unless a religious movement is demanding and different, it will not be taken seriously as a religious alternative. Movements must maintain a balance between conformity and deviation, and between innovation and continuity within a culture or social network.[20]

What did this medium tension look like for Wesley? Surprisingly, Wesley remained an Anglican his whole life. He loved the Anglican Church, and saw his Methodist societies as a renewal movement within Anglicanism. Methodism only became a separate denomination after his death.

As a movement, Methodism was free to act without the constraints of the Anglican system—able to attract committed followers who were alienated from the more respectable but lukewarm mainstream religion. And yet by remaining within Anglicanism, the Methodist societies were less likely to be seen as a deviant version of the Christian faith. They were distinct but connected to the culture around them. Methodism had the best of both worlds—high levels of member commitment *and* connection with the culture.

Researcher Christian Smith contrasts American evangelicalism with both fundamentalism and liberal Protestantism; he contends that what distinguishes evangelicalism is its "engaged orthodoxy." American evangelicals remain committed to orthodox Protestant theology and belief. At the same time, they confidently and proactively engage in the intellectual, cultural, social and political life of the nation. They are distinct *and* connected.[21]

In contrast, fundamentalism is a form of Protestantism that is defensively separate from the surrounding culture. It is distinct but not engaged. As a result, fundamentalism is a movement turned in on itself, lacking vitality. Liberal Protestants have chosen an even worse position; they are engaged with but not distinct from the prevailing culture. Their accommodation of the surrounding secular values lowers the tension with the culture but also weakens their ability to affect that culture. What remains for liberal Protestantism is the desire to reinterpret Christian faith with the categories, values and commitments of the modern/postmodern world.

The key to evangelicalism's vitality, then, is its ability to exist in tension with the surrounding culture while at the same time remaining engaged. Wesley maintained that tension; so did Jesus.

## JESUS AND COMMITMENT TO A CAUSE

*When Jesus calls a man, he bids him come and die!*

DIETRICH BONHOEFFER

At the beginning of his ministry Jesus proclaimed, "The time has come. . . . The kingdom of God is near. Repent and believe the good news!" (Mark 1:15). Jesus' cause was the kingdom of God. The establishment of God's rule through Jesus was good news because it brought healing to the sick, deliverance from Satan and demons, the offer of forgiveness and a new relationship with God as Father, and the promise of eternal life.[22]

Jesus called for a response of repentance and faith. The foundation of discipleship was personal commitment to him; self-denial was the fruit of that commitment. Jesus' disciples left everything and lived what might be called a "wartime" lifestyle. They left their occupations and their families. They called no town their home. They expected and experienced conflict and persecution. A sense of urgency kept Jesus and his followers moving from town to town as they announced and demonstrated the reality of God's rule.

What was Jesus' mission? Positively, he said that he came so that we might have life and have it to the full. He came into the world as a light so that anyone who believes in him should no longer live in darkness. He came to seek and save that which was lost.[23]

Yet his mission not only brought light, life and salvation, it also brought division and a sword. He came to bring fire on earth and longed for it to be kindled. He came to set a man against his father, a daughter against her mother, and a daughter-in-law against her mother-in-law. He came for judgment so that the blind would see, and those who can see would become blind.[24]

Jesus demonstrated unwavering commitment to his mission. Before launching his public ministry, he won a private battle against Satan's attempts to divert him from the true nature of his mission. He faced the continued scrutiny and opposition of the religious leaders. At the right time, he set his face to go to Jerusalem and die for the cause he championed. He died deserted by his closest companions.

Jesus expected the same unwavering commitment from his disciples. He expected his closest disciples to walk away from their livelihoods, to leave their homes behind and to follow him. Fishermen dropped their nets, tax collectors closed their books, and husbands and fathers left their homes. He told one young man to sell all he had, give it to the poor and follow him. Jesus challenged one disciple to choose between following him and burying his father.

On one occasion, when some of his followers became offended by his teaching and drifted away, he turned to the Twelve and asked, "You do not want to leave too, do you?" (John 6:67). Jesus' disciples were free to leave if he offended them, and he allowed for his disciples' mistakes and failures. But he never softened his call to total commitment to the cause of the kingdom. Jesus expected his followers to make the same sacrifices and demonstrate the same commitment that he did. Only those willing to take up their cross and follow him could be his disciples. Their loyalty to him had to come before every other loyalty. He told his disciples that he was sending them out as sheep to the wolves. They would be hated, persecuted and put in jail; some would even be killed. No disciple who turned back was worthy of him (see Matthew 10).

At the heart of Jesus' missionary movement were his closest disciples, who traveled and ministered with him and who were sent out on missions. They gave up their normal occupations and left their homes to join his mobile missionary team. A wider circle of up to five hundred people remained in their normal life situations, although some traveled with Jesus for short periods. Beyond them were the crowds of thousands, a mixture of opponents, onlookers, those seeking miracles and potential disciples. Jesus intentionally ministered within each of these concentric circles, but he made it his highest priority to intensively teach and train the few who made up the committed core of his movement.

Jesus left the expansion of the Christian movement to his followers, who were filled with his Holy Spirit for that purpose. The church that emerged after Pentecost both attracted and repelled people. In Jerusalem, in the wake of God's judgment on Ananias and Sapphira, no one else dared join with the followers of Jesus, even though they regarded them highly. Yet paradoxically, Luke records that increasing numbers of men and women believed in the Lord and were added to the church (Acts 5:13-15).

The people of Jerusalem were aware of a clear distinction between those who believed in Jesus and those who didn't. They knew that they too could join the movement at any time—but not without repentance and faith. There was something about the Jerusalem church that was attractive and at the same time dangerous.

The New Testament church had its share of failings, sins and heresies, yet no New Testament writer regarded this situation as acceptable. Paul admonished the Galatians for abandoning the gospel. He assigned anyone who preached another gospel to eternal condemnation. He warned the Corinthians not to indulge in idolatry and sexual immorality, or, like the Israelites, they would face God's judgment. Likewise, the writer of Hebrews called for perseverance under persecution and reminded his readers of the dangers of ignoring the discipline of God. Peter warned against false teachers in the church who were bringing destruction on themselves. John, in his epistle of love, wrote against those who had left the church and denied that Jesus is the Christ. He made it clear that those who deny the Son also deny the Father. He labeled those who teach such things as "antichrists." The book of Revelation begins with a series of letters to the churches with encouragements and warnings to stay true to the gospel in both doctrine and behavior. The risen Christ declares, "Those whom I love I rebuke and discipline. So be earnest, and repent" (Rev 3:19).[25]

Clearly, the church of the New Testament continued in the pattern that Jesus established of expecting faithfulness to the gospel in doctrine and behavior. There is grace and discipline for those who stray, but warnings, rebuke and expulsion for those who show contempt for the riches of God's kindness.

Jesus' call to discipleship clashes with every culture and every human heart. In the West, it confronts our modern/postmodern individualism. We are uncomfortable with a God who makes demands of us. We are uncomfortable with the idea that the Creator of the universe might have an opinion on how we should conduct ourselves. We recognize no other authority than ourselves. We do not easily come under the authority of the Scriptures or accountability to the body of Christ.

The call to commitment is hard for us to hear. It creates tension with the world around us. But both grace and truth are required to rescue a lost world.

## WHY SYDNEY ANGLICANS ARE UNPOPULAR

*What we suffer from today is humility in the wrong place. Modesty has moved from the organ of ambition. Modesty has settled upon the organ of conviction, where it was never meant to be. A man was meant to be*

*doubtful about himself, but undoubting about the truth; this has been
exactly reversed.*

G. K. CHESTERTON

Declining religious institutions sin by "omission"—it's what they
*don't* do that is the problem. Movements, by contrast, sin by "commission"; it's what they *do* that upsets everyone.

The Anglican diocese of Sydney is one of the most conservative
evangelical dioceses in the world. It has been that way since British settlement in 1788. Since then, as the rest of the Anglican
Church and Australian society have changed, Sydney Anglicans
have adapted their forms and methods but refuse to alter their
convictions about the truth of Scripture and the gospel.

One Anglican critic labeled them "fundamentalists" who are
narrow, rigid and ideological in their approach to life, the Scriptures and the church. An Anglican theologian described them as
"spiritually dangerous for the health of church and society" and
called them to repent of their narrow mindset.[26] This is one of the
indicators that Sydney Anglicans are a movement within Anglicanism; the strong reaction they provoke from the press and even from
other Anglicans. Movements clearly define who they are and have
an agenda for change. That brings them into tension with others.

There are more socially acceptable mainstream churches in
Australia than the Sydney Anglicans. Nobody is upset with them,
and nobody takes them seriously. Outside of the Sydney diocese,
Australian Anglicanism faces serious and worsening decline.
Half of all Anglican adult attenders are over sixty years old.[27]
Soon the largest age category for the Anglican church attenders
will be 70-79 years old. Members are dying, and they are not
being replaced.

In contrast with other dioceses, Sydney Anglicans are ordain-
ing record numbers of clergy and showing healthy growth in at-
tendance, new congregations and new churches. It seems ordinary

Australians respond well to these "dangerous fundamentalists." Whatever the future of Australian Christianity is, it will not be Anglican, unless it is Sydney Anglican.

What makes Sydney Anglicans different from other dioceses? At the heart it is their unwavering commitment to what they believe and their willingness to turn that belief into action. A good example is the Ministry Training Scheme (MTS), which offers apprenticeship training in Bible-centered ministry in churches across Australia. The stated purpose of MTS is "to train men and women who can declare the saving work of Christ in the world."[28] Participants are recruited from among the best young leaders in the dioceses. MTS looks for leaders who can break new ground for the gospel and train others to do the same. Classroom academics need not apply.

MTS takes both hands-on ministry and theological training seriously. Interns spend most of their time engaged in evangelism, youth ministry, leading conferences and camps, and teaching and pastoring small discipleship groups. They learn how to present the gospel both one-on-one and in small and large groups. Every intern is encouraged to start something new—ideally among non-Christians. MTS develops long-term partnerships with churches and pastors who provide apprentices with ministry experience, training and mentoring. Interns are paid a basic allowance by their church that enables them to commit to the program full time. Each week interns meet with a qualified pastor-trainer to review their ministry and reflect theologically. Pastor-trainers are chosen for their Bible-centered ministry and godly character. Many apprentices end up at the diocese's Moore Theological College, where they begin their formal theological education as experienced and proven practitioners. Eventually they return to the field and become recruiters and trainers of new interns.

By 2006 there were a thousand interns who had participated in the scheme; about 40 percent of them were women. In that year

240 interns were placed in 88 churches or university ministries. Graduates now serve in the media and arts, in education, as pastors and church planters, and as crosscultural missionaries in six different countries. No other diocese comes close to Sydney's achievement in growing the next generation of leaders. The price they pay for making a difference is that not everyone likes them.

## CONCLUSION

Commitment does not guarantee the rightness of a cause, but it does determine the likelihood of any cause making a difference. Committed people make history by living in alignment with their deeply held beliefs. Missionary movements build environments that sustain and reinforce commitment to the cause. They are in tension with the world around them because they have an agenda for change. They are also deeply connected with their world. It's the combination of connecting while remaining distinct that enables movements to make history.

# Contagious Relationships

*Every real friendship is a sort of secession, even a rebellion. . . . In each knot of Friends there is a sectional "public opinion" which fortifies its members against the public opinion of the community in general. Each therefore is a pocket of potential resistance.*

C. S. LEWIS

**M**y dad's boyhood hero was his older cousin, Jim Spence. Jim grew up in the Australian outback. With the outbreak of World War II looming, Jim and six of his mates lied about their ages and joined the Australian Army. Jim was sixteen.

When war broke out, the boys went into combat in North Africa. Later they were redeployed to fight in the jungles of New Guinea, an island to the north of Australia. As a young teenager, my father would eagerly await news of Jim's wartime adventures.

Out of all his friends, Jim was the only one to come home alive. He returned as a hero and moved to Sydney to live with Dad's family. Jim became like an older brother to Dad. On hot nights they slept out on the balcony under the stars and smoked Jim's army ration of tobacco.

All was not well with Jim. He was deeply disturbed by his horrific wartime experiences. He became depressed and thought about suicide. One Sunday afternoon Jim hit rock bottom. He had been drinking, and he decided he would jump off the Sydney Harbor Bridge. As he made his way toward the harbor, he could hear singing and music. An evangelist was preaching in the open air. Jim understood that only God could rescue him, and he put his trust in Jesus—much to the horror of my father!

By now Dad was eighteen. He had cruised through high school doing as little work as possible and getting into plenty of trouble. His one love was playing rugby. He could not understand or accept that his war-hero cousin had "gone religious." Jim invited Dad to different Christian meetings, but Dad wanted nothing to do with them.

A few months later Dad was in bed suffering from a bout of the mumps. Jim came to visit and challenged him about where his life was headed. Dad had witnessed the change in Jim, who was now planning to return to the jungles of New Guinea not as a soldier but as a missionary. Through Jim's example, my father became aware that his own life was lacking meaning and purpose.

Finally, Dad agreed to go with Jim to hear an American evangelist. That night Dad gave his life to Christ at the meeting. He began training to become a missionary, like Jim, to New Guinea. A few years later he completed theological training and married my mother. They sailed to New Guinea in 1951 as pioneer missionaries.

Jim spent the rest of his life as a missionary in New Guinea. After returning from missionary service, Dad spent the rest of his working life in ministry—first as a pastor in Australia then as the head of a Christian welfare agency.

Everything changed when Dad saw the transformation in Jim. Until then, Dad had no felt need for a faith of his own. Jim's dramatic conversion on the streets of Sydney is the exception. Dad's conversion through a close relationship is the rule. Like a virus, the gospel travels along these lines of preexisting contagious relationships.

## THE RISE OF CHRISTIANITY

*Finally, all questions concerning the rise of Christianity are one: How was it done? How did a tiny obscure messianic movement from the edge of the Roman Empire dislodge classical paganism and become the dominant faith of Western civilization?*

RODNEY STARK

We learn something about the nature of Christianity's expansion from one of the earliest recorded attacks on it. Celsus, a second-century Greek philosopher, alleged that Christianity was the faith of uneducated slaves, women and children. He complained it was spread from house to house "by wool workers, cobblers, laundry workers, and the most illiterate and bucolic yokels" who claimed that they alone knew the right way to live.[1]

In A.D. 30, seven weeks after the death and resurrection of Jesus, 120 men and women gathered in Jerusalem to wait and pray for the promised Holy Spirit. That day, the movement that Jesus founded was numbered in the hundreds. By the end of the day, it was thousands. By A.D. 66 there were around 40,000 followers throughout the Empire. By the end of the first century that number had grown to 100,000. By A.D. 300 the number had grown to around six million people, or about 10 percent of the population of the Roman Empire.[2] Christianity's spread was fast and spontaneous; it happened without a centralized coordinating organization. Only the Roman state rivaled Christianity in geographic spread and influence. Eventually, even Rome had to make its peace with Christianity.

Never has any movement—social, religious or political— achieved such a rapid advance in a dominant culture without the aid of military force. Not even the power of the Roman Empire could stamp out this new faith. How was it done?

In the first century, most Christians were Jewish, and their networks of friends and relatives were Jewish. If you had a church

gathering in your neighborhood, chances are you lived in a large
port city that was also home to a Jewish community—Alexan-
dria, Carthage, Corinth, Ephesus, Rome or Thessalonica.[3] Hellenistic Jews (Greek in language and culture) living outside of Israel were the most responsive people in the Empire to the
Christian gospel. They had weak ties to their traditional faith,
and they were open to new ideas. The apostle Paul fulfilled his
mission to the Gentiles by first reaching these Jews in Gentile
port cities. The network of Hellenistic synagogues throughout
the Empire was the beachhead through which the gospel spread
in depth.

What was true for Paul was also true of the great mass of ordinary Christians who spread the gospel throughout the Empire.
History has focused on the achievements of the leading figures of
the early church—apostles, prophets, teachers and evangelists
who played their part in knitting together a rapidly expanding
movement—but they were the exception, not the rule. Over-
whelmingly, early Christianity was not spread by "professionals"
but by ordinary people whose names and deeds went unrecorded.
Through their social networks of relatives and friends, they
reached the Hellenized Jews living outside Israel.

The Roman authorities sought to halt the expansion of Christianity by targeting its leadership. They assumed that if they
chopped off the head, the body would die. The pagan cults they
were used to dealing with were elitist organizations, supported by
the state and led by professional priests. The approach of targeting
Christian leaders did not work, however, because early Christianity was a mass movement with a highly committed rank and file
who were active in spreading the faith.[4]

Christian conversions followed networks of relationships. Missionaries often led the way, but their ministry focused on making
initial contacts with members of a social group. Once some insid-
ers were converted, they became the key to the gospel spreading

throughout the rest of the social network, while the missionary played a more supportive role.[5]

That's why Celsus complained that the new faith was spread from house to house by wool workers, cobblers, laundry workers, and illiterate and bucolic yokels. He was right to be concerned; the most reliable predictor of conversion is relationships, especially preexisting, positive relationships. No movement can sustain exponential growth if expansion is primarily the responsibility of paid professionals. Christianity grew exponentially as professional missionaries such as Paul supported and inspired the efforts of ordinary people.

Conversion is a social phenomenon; it is often about accepting the faith of one's friends.[6] Whatever someone's prior beliefs, he is far more likely to adopt a new faith if he witnesses a friend or family member convert to that faith. As the number of recently converted friends and family increases, so does the likelihood of conversion.[7]

As open movements grow, their "social surface" expands exponentially. Each new member opens up new networks of relationships between the movement and potential members.[8] For continued exponential growth, a movement must maintain such open relationships with outsiders, and it must also reach out into new, adjacent social networks. Contagious relationships are at the heart of the spread of every movement; when new religious movements become closed social networks, they fail.

Early Christianity grew because converts maintained open relationships with the social worlds from which they came. If the church had responded to persecution and ridicule by becoming a closed, secretive sect, there is no way it could have continued to win new converts. Instead, the Christian faith continued to spread into adjacent social networks.[9]

The importance of social networks is true for the spread of all faiths, but Christianity had an advantage, inherited from Judaism—belief in one true God. In ancient Rome no one supposed that there was only one valid religion or only one true God, so there were no missionaries. Nor was there such a thing as "conversion." When there are many gods, new gods are added without the need to reject old ones; they function as "supplements rather than alternatives." Only monotheism can generate the level of commitment to mobilize nonprofessionals in evangelism.[10]

Nonexclusive religions cater to individualistic consumers who can choose from an array of options. Without monotheism, it is very difficult to build a communal faith with social strength. That's why paganism in the Greco-Roman culture had difficulty in getting anyone to do anything. There was no "church" of paganism. There was no missionary enterprise to take the "good news" of paganism to the ends of the earth. In contrast, Christianity was able to channel members' commitment into building Christian community and taking the message of salvation to the world.

Like Christianity, Judaism was also a monotheistic faith, but it never matched Christianity in reaching Gentiles. To fully convert to the Jewish faith, Gentiles had to become Jews; in contrast, Christianity appealed to both Jews and Gentiles, Greeks and barbarians, men and women, slaves and free. It reached the poor and the ignorant, as well as the educated and the wealthy, with the simple message of the gospel.

Christianity appealed to all levels of society, and it spread rapidly through relational networks. The resulting intense community of followers, committed to a common cause, proved more powerful than the state-sponsored religions and even more powerful than the might of Empire. Christianity ultimately conquered the Roman world without an organizational structure, without access to significant resources, without academic institutions and without a professionalized clergy. Ordinary people, on fire with the love of Christ and empowered by the Holy Spirit, simply told their families, friends and casual acquaintances what God had done for them.

By the fourth century, Rome had a Christian emperor in Constantine. Christianity came to occupy a position of privilege, backed by the Roman state. The church gained the power and resources it lacked, but it lost the intense commitment and missionary zeal of its members.

## PRINCIPLES OF CONTAGIOUS RELATIONSHIPS

Belief is a social phenomenon. Whether you're a communist, a Manchester United fan, a conservative or an environmentalist, relationships play an important part in forming and maintaining your beliefs. Ideas spread like viruses, from person to person. In the age of mass communication, word of mouth is still the most important form of communication. Relationships are the key ingredient in the exponential growth of movements.

Movements appear to grow spontaneously and randomly, but on closer inspection they are spreading within and across networks of relationships. A study in the 1970s of American Pentecostalism showed that this movement was growing via face-to-face recruitment within preexisting social networks. Wives came to faith when they saw the change in their husbands. Young adults converted soon after the conversion of a long-term friend. The stronger the social network, the faster Pentecostalism spread upon gaining a foothold. In contrast, communities made up of disconnected individuals were unlikely to see rapid growth.[11]

There are many factors that influence the decision to adopt a new faith, but the most important factor is a close and positive relationship with a committed participant.[12] From a human point of view, conversion is accepting the opinion of your friends.[13] Mass meetings and dynamic leaders are not enough for effective recruitment, unless they play a role in motivating existing members to win over their social networks. The key to the spread of any movement is face-to-face recruitment by committed participants.[14]

For a movement to grow rapidly it has to spread both *within* and *between* social networks. Successful movements develop strategies to remain open social networks that are able to reach into new adjacent social networks. Here are three factors that contribute to how contagious a movement becomes.

*The strength of weak ties.* If you're looking for a job, forget about searching newspapers and the Internet; you should get out and meet people. You're most likely to get your next job through your relationships—possibly through a friend, but more likely through an acquaintance. This phenomenon is called "the strength of weak ties."[15] Your close friends tend to link you with people you already know. By contrast, acquaintances link you to a variety of untapped social networks. They expand your relational world. Movements rarely spend vast amounts of money on advertising and mass communication, intuitively favoring the more relational expansion that weak ties support.

Certain people act as the links within and between social networks. Malcolm Gladwell classifies these people as *connectors*, *mavens* and *salesmen*.[16] Connectors have an extraordinary ability to make multiple friends and acquaintances across different networks. With a foot in so many different relational worlds, they bring people together. Connectors are people specialists, while mavens (Yiddish for someone who accumulates knowledge) are information specialists—the people you go to when you need information to make a decision. They love accumulating knowledge and communicating it to others. Salesmen, meanwhile, are persuaders; they connect emotionally with others and convince them of the need to adopt new ideas or behaviors. These three types of people are the bridges over which new ideas spread contagiously from person to person and group to group.

*Tight but open social networks.* For a movement to grow, it must not only reach new people, it must retain them *and* build them into a committed force for change. To do so, it is important to foster strong relationships *within* the movement. Movements made up of a collection of casual acquaintances will lack energy, commitment and focus. A successful movement is a "tight" social network.

Yet, if a movement is too tight, it will become socially isolated; it may keep its members, but it will not grow. In closed groups, internal relationships can be so strong that they exclude significant relationships with outsiders. This social isolation limits the ability to recruit, and those who *are* recruited will tend to be isolated individuals without strong social networks—unlikely to be the relational bridge that others cross to join the movement.

Growth can only continue if the movement remains a tight *and* open social network.[17] Effective movements maintain a balance between internal and external attachments. They retain the ability to reach out and into new adjacent social networks. By doing so, they are able to sustain exponential rates of growth.[18]

*Just six handshakes away.* In 1967 social psychologist Stanley Milgram asked his students at Harvard to help him find out how many acquaintances it takes to connect two randomly selected people.[19] Two names were chosen, and each student received a letter with the instructions:

• If you are acquainted with the person, mail it directly to them

• If not, mail it to someone you know personally who is more likely than you to know the target.

• Have them do the same.

Milgram and his students discovered that the most common number of intermediate persons was 5.5. In 1991 John Guare turned the idea into a play called *Six Degrees of Separation*. Despite the complexity of our world, we are all just a few handshakes away from everyone else. Movements are social organisms more than they are organizations; their organizing structure is formed by overlapping networks of relationships. That should be no surprise, since God is Father, Son and Holy Spirit. God has made us, in his image, as social beings.

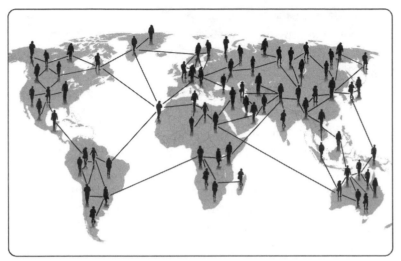

**Figure 3.1.** We are just six handshakes away from everyone on the planet.

## JESUS AND CONTAGIOUS RELATIONSHIPS

*The first thing Andrew did was to find his brother Simon and tell him,*
*"We have found the Messiah."*

JOHN 1:41

Jesus knew the importance of relationships. From the beginning, the movement he founded grew through the favorable reports that spread from person to person.

Jesus recruited his band of disciples through relational networks. It was John the Baptist, Jesus' relative, who first connected Jesus to Andrew; Andrew went and found his brother Simon Peter to tell him he had met the Messiah. Jesus called Philip, who was from Bethsaida, Andrew and Peter's town. Philip, recruited Nathaniel, and James and John were fishermen together with Peter and Andrew.

Jesus turned individual encounters into opportunities to touch whole social networks. The Gerasene demoniac begged Jesus to be allowed to join his band of disciples. Instead, Jesus told him to go home and tell his family what God had done (Mk 5). Soon after Levi became a disciple, Jesus and the Twelve were at Levi's house for a great banquet with Levi's friends who were tax collectors and "sinners" (Lk 5). When Jesus met Zacchaeus, his ultimate aim was not just to reach Zacchaeus but also his family and friends. Jesus announced, "Today salvation has come to this house" (Lk 19:9). Jesus moved from village to village looking for responsive people who would take the good news into the world of their relationships. He built longer-term relationships with his disciples, but he had a harvest model of evangelism. Always on the move, he scattered the seed of the gospel broadly and then watched it multiply through others.

Jesus warned of the power of relationships as a hindrance to faith: "If anyone comes to me and does not hate his father and mother, his wife and children, his brothers and sisters—yes, even his own life— he cannot be my disciple" (Lk 14:26). He sent out his disciples with the instructions to look for a "person of peace" wherever they went— a well-known person of the community who was receptive to the messengers and the message. The disciples on mission had no relational contacts of their own; the person of peace became the bridge into the community's social networks (see Lk 10).

This pattern of reaching households and relationship networks continued in the book of Acts. When the gospel spread to the Gentiles, the entry point was through Cornelius, who gathered his relatives and close friends to hear Peter preach (Acts 10). At Philippi, Lydia and her household believed and were baptized. Later Paul and Silas challenged the Philippian jailer and his whole family to believe and be baptized (Acts 16). In Corinth, Crispus, the synagogue ruler, and his entire household believed (Acts 18). In his letters to the churches, Paul often referred to whole households that had been won to Christ, including "the first converts in Achaia"—the household of Stephanas (1 Cor 16:15). Throughout the New Testament, the key for the spread of the gospel is contagious relationships.

## MULTIPLYING ORGANIC CHURCHES

Neil Cole is a church planter with a difference. In his first year of church planting in Long Beach, California, he and his coworkers started ten new churches. The next year, teams from those new churches started eighteen additional churches; the following year the network planted fifty-two churches. In 2002 this growing network planted 106 new churches. After six years they had planted around 800 churches across the United States and in twenty-three nations. Neil's Awakening Chapels and the church networks they have spun off have continued to multiply. There are even great-great-grandparent churches that have spawned five generations of new churches.

Neil's new churches were small (averaging sixteen people) and simple, because small, simple things are easier to reproduce. These "organic" churches spring up where life happens. Church happens wherever the seed of the gospel is planted.[20] He has churches meeting in coffeehouses, businesses and homes. There are churches that reach out to people in Twelve-Step recovery groups and to the people in local bars. They reach out to homosexuals, occult groups, neighborhood gangs, the homeless, and high school and college students.

Neil says that if you saw a hand sticking up out of the sand of a beach and waving for help, you would assume there is a body attached to it that needs air.[21] When Neil's coworkers go into a new area, he advises them to look for a "person of peace" within a social network. The person of peace—someone who is receptive to the gospel, is well connected relationally and has a good (or bad) reputation—becomes a conduit for the passing of the message of the kingdom to an entire community of lost people. The person's reputation gives credence to the message and becomes a magnet for the new church.

Neil calls this phenomenon the "first domino principle" and identifies it in the New Testament. In the Gospels the Samaritan woman at the well did not have a good reputation. Neither did the Gerasene demoniac, but when their lives were turned around, they each became a witness to their community. In the book of Acts, both Lydia and Cornelius had good reputations. Their witness was also effective.

One of Neil's "first dominos" ran a painting business in Long Beach, California. Michael was a drug addict, and his house was a constant party. But the drugs gradually took over his life, and he lost his truck, his business and his wife. After he gave his life to Christ, God graciously gave him back everything—and more. Now instead of running a party house, he and his wife, Carlita, host a church in their home. Fifteen to twenty people attend regularly.

Over six years this small fellowship birthed twenty new churches. These believers have sent out church planters across the United States and to France, Jordan, Kosovo and North Africa. Michael and Carlita are always reaching new people and always sending people out to start new churches around the corner, across the nation and in faraway places. Michael has learned to allow the gospel to follow and spread through relational worlds; he has also learned to teach new believers to do the same.

## CONCLUSION

There is no faster or more cost effective way for an idea, a fashion or a rumor to spread than from person to person and group to group. Technology can never replace the power of face-to-face recruitment by committed participants. Jesus understood the importance of relationships, and so did his followers.

It does not take vast amounts of money to fill a nation with the knowledge of the gospel. What it takes is ordinary people, on fire with the love of Christ and empowered by the Holy Spirit, who are willing to tell their families, friends and casual acquaintances what God has done for them.

# Rapid Mobilization

*The best time to plant a tree was twenty years ago. The second best
time is today.*

CHINESE PROVERB

**A** **few years ago, we hired** some workers to build an extension on
our home. A year later I caught up with our contractor, Des Nixon,
over coffee and pancakes. Here's how the conversation went:

"Des, I hear you're building hospitals and factories these days.
Are you getting out of building houses?"

"I don't build buildings, Steve."

"Well, what do you do? You're a builder!"

"I build builders."

You could have knocked me over with a house brick. Over the
next hour I learned more about growing leaders than I had in my
many years of formal training for the ministry. I discovered Des's
mission in life was not to be a builder; it was to grow young men.

At our local church, Des had a ministry of discipling young
men. He was smart enough to know that you don't do that sitting
around in someone's living room. So he piled them into his four-
wheel-drive vehicle, and off they went into the Australian desert

for a week. Some of the young men had troubled backgrounds. Others no longer had fathers around. As God worked in these young men's lives, Des began thinking that he would like to give some of them a job.

Previously Des had no intention of growing his business. He was happy working on his own. Today, however, Des has a team of eighteen men working for him. A number of them have come to know Christ through him.

Here's how Des builds builders:

*Recruit.* Des's first workers came through his ministry to young men in his local church. He spent time with them. He took them away on camping trips. Some came from established and stable church families; others from troubled backgrounds. As Des developed a reputation for turning boys into men, people sent others to him. Pastors, parents, other builders, even his own children would recommend young men who were looking for work and for direction. Now Des doesn't need to actively recruit; they come to him.

*Select.* Before he hires anyone, Des prays and asks God if he should hire this particular young man. If the answer is yes, he employs him for two to three months as a casual laborer. Then Des watches—and his supervisors watch—and the other workers watch. They want to see if this new guy is willing to learn. Does he embrace the company's values of honesty, integrity, fun and commitment to relationships?

Des has created a culture. Most new workers mature quickly through being in an environment where they are valued and respected and where people have high expectations of each other. After two to three months, the team knows if someone will make it.

*Grow.* Once a worker has proved himself, Des takes him on as an apprentice, and the real learning begins. Des sets standards that are higher than what the government expects. He will even pay an apprentice's wages while he works for two months with another carpenter who is skilled in a particular aspect of the trade. Des wants his apprentices to learn from the best.

*Multiply*. After an apprentice has finished his training with Des, he can stay on and work as a qualified carpenter. He then becomes eligible to become a supervisor. Des has seven supervisors. He meets with them regularly and shares everything about the business with them. When a difficulty arises, he draws them into the process of resolving it. They experience firsthand how much he values honesty, even when he has to pay a price for it.

Supervisors begin by quoting on and running smaller jobs; as they gain experience, they graduate to larger ones. Des stays in the background and helps his supervisors grow through the challenge. His goal is that 50 percent of his carpenters will become supervisors and go on to become builders who run their own businesses.

*Sustain*. It doesn't sound like good business sense to turn half your qualified workforce into future competitors—until you ask Des how business is going. During one recent financial year his company grew by over 40 percent. His clients are happy, his workers love him and the business is healthy. Des does not pursue profits; he pursues his mission profitably.

Des's mission is to grow young men. He lives by the conviction that if he fulfills his mission, God will look after his business. In ten years Des is planning to get out of the building trade and spend the rest of his life in the background, encouraging the men he has grown. Des Nixon is a movement leader. He knows the principles and practices better than most church leaders I know.

In the previous chapter we saw that no missionary movement can grow exponentially if its expansion is solely the responsibility of paid professionals. Movements spread, rather, through the efforts of ordinary people who inspire and equip key leaders.

## HOW THE WEST WAS WON

*It is hard to imagine any sum of money that would have caused an Anglican Bishop to travel nearly 300,000 miles on horseback as Francis Asbury did, disregarding weather and chronic ill health, "to goad his men and to supervise their work."*

ROGER FINKE AND RODNEY STARK

When the twenty-six-year-old Methodist pioneer Francis Asbury arrived in the American colonies in 1771, he believed he was called to fulfill a great destiny. He was right—although that destiny was far greater than he ever imagined.[1] In 1771 there were only three hundred American Methodists, led by four ministers. By the time of Asbury's death in 1816, Methodism had two thousand ministers and over 200,000 members in a well-coordinated movement. By 1830 official membership was almost half a million, and the number of actual attenders was six million. Most of these people had no previous church connection before they became Methodists.[2]

Asbury, like his mentor John Wesley, modeled the commitment required to achieve such success. Throughout his ministry Asbury delivered more than 16,000 sermons. He traveled nearly 300,000 miles on horseback. He remained unmarried so that he could devote himself fully to his mission. He was often ill and had no permanent home. He was paid the salary of an ordinary traveling preacher and was still traveling when he died at seventy years of age.

Asbury's leadership and example inspired an army of circuit riders, many of whom followed his example and remained unmarried. There were no formal vows, but in the early days of the movement the majority of the riders lived by the three rules of the monastic orders: poverty, chastity and obedience. Methodism was a kind of Protestant missionary order under one leader, adapted to reaching isolated communities in harsh conditions across an entire nation.[3]

Jacob Young, a typical circuit rider, was twenty-six years old in 1802 when he took up the challenge of pioneering a Methodist circuit along the Green River in Kentucky. Young developed his own strategy to evangelize the region. He would travel five miles, find a settlement and look for a family who would let him preach in their log cabin to interested friends and neighbors. Sometimes he found groups already gathered, waiting for a preacher to arrive; in one location he discovered a society run by an illiterate African American slave with impressive preaching and leadership skills. Young established class meetings wherever he went, to be run by local leaders in his absence.

Circuit riders like Jacob Young began with limited formal education, but they followed the example of Wesley and Asbury and used their time on horseback for study. They spoke the simple language of the frontier. They faced ridicule, and even violence, with courage and endurance. Above all else they sought conversions. Within a year of his call, Young had gathered 301 new members; for his efforts he received just $30—a cost of ten cents per new member.[4]

In 1776 only 17 percent of the American population was affiliated with any church. By 1850 that number had doubled to 34 percent. Most of the growth was as a result of the gains by the Methodists and Baptists on the frontier. Francis Asbury could never have reached a nation as vast as the United States, no matter how many miles he rode, no matter how many sermons he preached, without rapidly mobilizing young circuit riders like Jacob Young.

The Protestant mainline denominations (Episcopalians, Presbyterians and Congregationalists) failed dismally to keep pace with these Baptist and Methodist upstarts. Having succumbed to a more settled version of the faith and having lost the zeal for evangelism, the message of the mainline denominations became too vague and too accommodating to have an impact.

The clergy of the mainline churches were well educated and refined, drawn from the social elites. At least 95 percent of Congregational, Episcopalian and Presbyterian ministers were college graduates, compared to only 10 percent of the Baptists. As a combined group the mainline denominations had trained six thousand ministers before the first Methodist minister graduated from a seminary.

Higher education lifted the mainline clergy above the social status of their congregations and turned them into religious professionals. Secularized theological education and social background influenced both the content of their message and how it was delivered. The clergy preferred to educate their hearers rather than convert them. The clergy's carefully drafted scholarly sermons did little to stir hearts; they were out of touch with the common people. There also weren't enough of them; it was not possible to mobilize enough well-educated, well-paid clergy to respond to the challenge of the rapidly expanding frontier. If expansion had been left to the older denominations, American Christianity may have ended up today looking more like the church of Europe—theologically refined, but declining.[5]

So the mainline clergy watched from the safety of the larger towns and cities along the Atlantic seaboard while the Baptists and Methodists moved west. On the frontier it was hard to tell Methodist and Baptist preachers apart. They were ordinary folk with limited education. They spoke the language of the people and preached from the heart about the need for salvation from sin. As they preached, the power of God was not only spoken about, it was experienced. Methodist pioneer Peter Cartwright recalled that "while I was preaching, the power of God fell on the assembly and there was an awful shaking among the dry bones. Several fell on the floor and cried for mercy."[6]

The Baptists and the Methodists developed strategies that made it easy for gifted and committed laypeople to take up leadership and go where the people and the opportunities were. Deployment was rapid because very little upfront investment of resources and education was required. Methodist preachers, many of whom were teenagers, were trained on the job as "apprentices" by more experienced workers. They were expected to be continually studying as they traveled. They practiced lifelong learning and graduated the day they died.

The Methodists were centrally governed, whereas the Baptists believed in local autonomy. But in actuality, both movements planted self-governing congregations. The Methodist circuit riders did not have the time to settle down in one place and take control. Their role was to pioneer new works and mobilize local workers to continue the ministry in depth. These self-governing congregations were well suited to rapid multiplication in the frontier culture.

Methodism gave unprecedented freedom to both women and African Americans to engage in ministry.[7] Methodist preachers called the converted to join a growing movement and offered them the opportunity to make a significant contribution—as class leaders, lay preachers or even circuit riders. Some women served as preachers, and many more served as class leaders, unofficial counselors to the circuit riders, network builders and financial patrons. Large numbers of African American Methodist preachers emerged following the Revolutionary War. Some were well-known public figures. Harry Hosier, probably born a slave, traveled with Asbury and other Methodist leaders and preached to large crowds, both white and black. Methodists and Baptists, unlike the established churches, preached in a way uneducated slaves could understand and affirmed the place of spiritual experiences and emotion. African American preachers played a significant role in shaping the Methodist movement.

The Baptists and Methodists flourished because they mobilized common people to preach the gospel and plant churches wherever

there was a need. The Presbyterians, Episcopalians and Congregationalists languished because they were controlled by well-paid
clergy who were recruited from the social and financial elite. Early
growth was dramatic for the Methodists—from 2.5 percent of the
church-going population in 1776 to 34 percent in 1850, with four
thousand itinerant preachers, almost eight thousand local preachers and over one million members.[8] This made them by far the
largest religious body in the nation. There was only one national
institution that was more extensive—the U.S. government. This
achievement would have been impossible without the mobilization of ordinary people—white and black, young and old, men
and women—and the removal of artificial barriers to their engagement in significant leadership as class leaders, local workers
and itinerant preachers. Unfortunately, the Methodist rise was
short-lived. Whereas before 1840 the Methodists had virtually
no college-educated clergy among their circuit riders and local
preachers,[9] their amateur clergy were gradually replaced by
seminary-educated professionals who claimed the authority of the

**Table 2. Adherents per 1000 population for Methodist and Baptist denom-
inational families, 1776-1980.** Roger Finke and Rodney Stark, *The Churching of
America, 1776-1990: Winners and Losers in Our Religious Economy* (New Brunswick, N.J.: Rutgers University Press, 1992), p. 146.

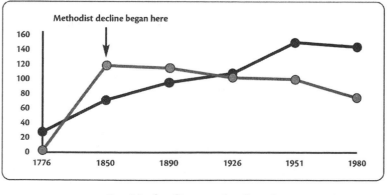

church hierarchy over their congregations.[10] Their relative slump began at the same time; by the end of the nineteenth century the Baptists had overtaken them in numbers.

## THE SPONTANEOUS EXPANSION OF THE CHURCH

*The Church was first established and organized with a worldwide mission for a world-wide work. It was a living organism composed of living souls deriving their life from Christ, who was its Head. It was an organism which grew by its own spontaneous activity, the expression of that life which it had in union with Christ, the Savior.*

ROLAND ALLEN

Roland Allen was an Anglican missionary to northern China around the turn of the twentieth century. His mission experience and his study of Paul's ministry led him to a radical reassessment of Western missionary theology and practice. He looked for the factors that accompanied the spontaneous expansion of the gospel and wrote about their significance. Through his study of the book of Acts, Allen saw the church as a living organism that grows spontaneously through its union with Christ. The church's missionary activity does not come from ecclesiastical control but from the spontaneous, individual activity of its members who are led by the Holy Spirit.[11]

According to Allen, spontaneous expansion is *inhibited* under these conditions:

1. When paid foreign professionals are primarily responsible to spread the gospel, causing the gospel to be seen as an alien intrusion.

2. When the church is dependent on foreign funds and leadership. Allen asked, "How can a man propagate a religion which he cannot support and which he cannot expect those whom he addresses to be able to support?"

3. When the spread of the gospel is controlled out of fear of error, and both error and godly zeal are suppressed.

4. When it is believed that the church is to be founded, educated, equipped and established in the doctrine, ethics and organization before it is to expand.

5. When emerging leaders are restricted from ministering until they are fully trained and so learn the lesson of inactivity and dependency.

6. When conversion is seen as the result of clever argument rather than the power of Christ.

7. When professional clergy control the ministry and discourage the spontaneous zeal of nonprofessionals. They may protect the new believers from charlatans like Simon the magician (Acts 8:9-24), but in doing so they also block unconventional leaders like Peter the fisherman.[12]

According to Allen, spontaneous expansion is *enhanced* under these conditions:

1. When new converts immediately tell their story to those who know them.

2. When, from the beginning, evangelism is the work of those within the culture.

3. When true doctrine results from the true experience of the power of Christ rather than mere intellectual instruction. Heresies are not produced by ignorance but by the speculations of learned men.

4. When the church is self-supporting and provides for its own leaders and facilities.

5. When new churches are given the freedom to learn by experience and are supported but not controlled. Allen believed the great things of God are beyond human control. He observed

that control produces sterility. Controlled converts may not go astray, but they produce nothing.

Allen was committed to harnessing the potential of ordinary people and the power of the Holy Spirit for the spread of indigenous church planting movements. A century later, Allen's views have been confirmed by the vibrancy of Christianity in the "global South"—the developing world of the southern hemisphere. According to historian Philip Jenkins, that vibrancy confounds the myth that Christianity is a European American religion exported to a passive Third World. Over the past two centuries, the Christianity first kindled around the world by European missionaries "soon turned into an uncontrollable bushfire."[13]

Missionaries have an image in the West as religious imperialists. Yet their remarkable success, according to Jenkins, was not due to the imposition of a foreign faith backed with political and economic power. They succeeded where the church that was planted in fresh soil adapted to local circumstances and took on a life of its own. Leadership roles, especially in the Pentecostal and independent churches, are not restricted to those who have been formally trained in Western-oriented academic institutions. Local leaders are chosen who demonstrate the required spiritual gifts and qualities. Christianity has flourished when it is no longer dependent on foreign leadership, funding and control.[14]

## JESUS AND RAPID MOBILIZATION

*When they saw the courage of Peter and John and realized that they were unschooled, ordinary men, they were astonished and they took note that these men had been with Jesus.*

ACTS 4:13

At the beginning of his ministry, Jesus recruited disciples with the promise that he would teach them how to catch people rather than fish. He refused to entrust himself to the crowds, but he entrusted himself to his disciples. Jesus reached the multitudes, but his purpose was to grow the leaders who would continue his ministry in the power of the Holy Spirit.

Jesus called a select band of followers to leave their work and even their families to be with him. Simon and Andrew left their nets, James and John left their boat and their father Zebedee, and Matthew-Levi left his lucrative position as a tax collector. These became Jesus' constant companions and coworkers in a mobile missionary band.

Fishermen and tax collectors without formal religious training were excluded from serving in the temple, they were excluded from membership in the ruling council of the Sanhedrin, and they were excluded from joining the Pharisees.[15] Jesus chose these ordinary men because they wanted to follow him. Jesus invested his life in training them, and he entrusted the movement he founded to them.

What form did the disciples' training take? To teach them about faith, Jesus led them into a dangerous storm. He sent them out on mission trips to teach them to trust God for their needs and to learn how to preach, heal the sick and cast out demons. They learned how to pray by watching him pray and hearing him teach about prayer. Jesus threw them together in a mobile missionary community and taught them lessons about authority and humility. They watched Jesus' clashes with the Pharisees and learned how to deal with opposition. Jesus' training of the Twelve fused content and context.

Jesus' teaching was obedience oriented. His model of training assumed that the disciples did not know something until they had learned to obey it. He trained the head, the heart, and the hands of his disciples and expected them to pass on what they learned to others. At the end of their apprenticeship, Jesus told his disciples it was good that he was going away because the Spirit would come to lead them into all truth and empower them to be witnesses to the world.

The gospel and the power of the Holy Spirit were the guarantees of the disciples' authority and effectiveness in mission. The Word and the Spirit enabled the early disciples to confidently release others into the proclamation of the gospel and the planting of new churches. Early Christianity advanced through the efforts of ordinary people. In the New Testament there is no distinction between "clergy" and "laity." Every disciple of Christ is ordained for ministry.[16] There were "professional" missionaries like the Twelve, Philip, Barnabas and Paul, but the great bulk of missionary work was carried out by unknown and unnamed "amateurs," both men and women.

Paul, like Jesus, functioned as the leader of a missionary band. There are around one hundred names in Acts and the Epistles of different people associated with Paul.[17] He refers to thirty-six of them with terms like "brother," "apostle," "fellow-worker" and "servant." Of these, nine coworkers are in close association with Paul. He frequently traveled and ministered with others such as Barnabas, John Mark, Silas, Timothy and Luke. In his letters, he often mentions his fellow workers such as Timothy, Epaphroditus and Luke. He regularly tells his readers that he is sending a team member to them for a particular purpose.[18] Some of Paul's letters bear not just his name as the sender, but also the names of some of his team members. Philippians comes from "Paul and Timothy." Galatians comes from Paul and "all the brothers with me."

Paul expected the churches he planted to reach their region in depth and to become partners with him in his missionary enterprise through prayer, giving and releasing workers. He congratulated the Thessalonians that "the Lord's message rang out from you not only in Macedonia and Achaia—your faith in God has become known everywhere" (1 Thess 1:8). He thanked the Philippians for their "partnership in the gospel" (Phil 1:5).

There can be no doubt that Jesus founded a missionary movement, expanded by Paul, that grew through ordinary people who were trained—head, heart and hands—in the context of everyday life and ministry. What could it look like if we followed this example today?

## RALPH MOORE AND THE HOPE CHAPEL MOVEMENT

*We're not smart. We're just relentless.*

RALPH MOORE

In the Western world some churches and denominations are planting churches, but very few are multiplying them. That's why Ralph Moore and the Hope Chapel movement caught my attention.[19] Ralph Moore was twenty-five years old in 1972 when he planted the first Hope Chapel in Manhattan Beach, California. He had a wife and an infant son. His hair was short, and he wore a three-piece suit at a time when everyone else had long hair and wore jeans. He had no guaranteed income and a car with 154,000 miles on the clock. Like most church planters, he had more faith than sense.

When I spent time with Ralph in 2008, he recalled how that church began with just enough people to fill a Volkswagen Beetle. Soon it grew to twenty, including several bikers, a Marine corporal, a newborn baby and a topless dancer. By the time the new church had 125 people, it had planted a daughter church.

In 1983 Ralph moved to Hawaii to plant another church. The new church began under a tree in a park by the beach. By 2000, Hope Chapel Kaneohe Bay had grown to 1,600 people and had planted sixty churches.

One of the new Christians in Hawaii was Mel Isara. He became a pastor of a "MiniChurch" (Hope Chapel's primary unit for pastoral care and disciple making) and began multiplying other groups. Mel caught Ralph's vision for church planting and planted his first church in 2001. Six months into the plant he stood up in front of the congregation and told them he was leaving in two years; he then introduced the man he was training to be their pastor.

Mel's next church plant was in a tough neighborhood. At the first church service, Mel told the congregation he would be the laziest pastor they had ever met because he was going to equip them to do the ministry. He also announced he would be leaving in two-and-a-half years and introduced their future pastor: "Junior," a former alcoholic and drug addict whom Mel had been equipping for the previous four years. Junior had already multiplied five MiniChurches and was ready to become a pastor. In March 2005 Mel fulfilled his promise to hand the church over to Junior and then left to plant a third church in Pearl City, Hawaii.

Ralph Moore believes that church must be simple and it must reproduce. He intentionally names his small groups MiniChurches and their leaders "undershepherds." MiniChurches meet weekly to review the Bible teaching from the weekend services. The format is simple and reproducible:

*What did you learn?* (head)
*What did God say to you?* (heart)
*What will you do?* (hands)

The MiniChurch is the building block for the local church; it is also the farm system for future leaders. Faithful group members who are influencing others are recruited as apprentice leaders and trained. Faithful apprentices become MiniChurch pastors. MiniChurch pastors who are effective in multiplying groups and leaders are invited to join a "Pastor Factory." They meet weekly to read and discuss books on leadership and theology. The training is built on the same model of head, heart and hands. They start and grow two to three MiniChurches and then take those people with them to plant a church.

Hope Chapel church planters are not theological seminary graduates but disciples who can make disciples. Many of them have come to faith through the movement and have grown into leadership in the local church. Ralph believes that only a small percentage of those who enter traditional theological training make it through graduation and survive more than two years of pastoral ministry. Theological education in its current form creates barriers to entry into ministry. Hope Chapel, by contrast, combines learning, ministry assignments and mentoring to grow hundreds of leaders, and over 90 percent of them have remained in the ministry. Ralph contends that education cannot create a leader, it can only augment and improve one. Theological learning should be integrated with an active engagement in ministry. The local church should be the "seminary" that trains church planters and pastors.

Ralph believes growing leaders is like training baseball players. Players need plenty of opportunities to swing the bat; they also need a willingness to learn from their mistakes. MiniChurches give future leaders a chance to swing the bat in a low-risk environment. They are then given feedback and coaching. How does Ralph know if someone is a leader? He watches to see if anyone is following them.

Since 1972 Ralph has seen over seven hundred churches, small and large, started in North America and the Asia-Pacific region. Many of those churches are now themselves parents, grandparents, great-grandparents and even great-great-grandparents of new churches. If Ralph had planted a church in Hawaii that grew to ten thousand people, he'd be world famous. Instead, he planted a church that multiplies churches, together amounting to seventy thousand people. Ralph has formed a culture of believing in mavericks and of providing challenging environments in which they can grow. Ralph's a great guy, and I hope he lives a long and fruitful life, but if he died tomorrow the movement he has inspired would continue to advance.

## CONCLUSION

Whether it is Des Nixon or Francis Asbury or Ralph Moore, great leaders grow leaders. They reject the arrogant notion that their ministry is primary. Like Jesus, great leaders create opportunities that equip and mobilize others. They focus on the whole person: hands, head and heart. And they don't just grow leaders, they *multiply* them. They know the harvest is plentiful and the workers are few. They have learned that if the eternal Son of God spent the bulk of his precious time growing leaders, they should do the same.

# 5

# Adaptive Methods

*In a time of drastic change, it is the learners who inherit the future.*
*The learned find themselves equipped to live in a world that no longer*
*exists.*

ERIC HOFFER

**In 1974 I finished my final year** of high school and immediately flew out for the western highlands of Papua New Guinea, an island to the north of Australia. The purpose of the trip was to help build an airstrip in a remote mountain village whose inhabitants had had contact with Europeans for less than ten years.

A few days after we arrived in the village, men from over the mountain walked through the night and arrived early in the morning to challenge the men of our village to a contest. A round object was placed on the ground between the opposing tribes, and for the next two and a half hours, fifty men battled to land the ball between two posts sunk into the ground at each end. They were playing soccer, or as most of the world calls it, "football." It was wild, chaotic and fun, but it was still soccer.

At the end of the morning the players broke for a meal of sweet potatoes and bananas, and they rested briefly before resuming the game in the afternoon. That evening all the men sat around the fire, eating roast pig and sweet potatoes and singing their way through the night. Before dawn the visitors left for home, singing as they went. Quite an improvement from tribal warfare!

Different forms of soccer have been played for thousands of years in diverse cultures. In the Han Dynasty, the Chinese game was called *cuju*, and it involved kicking a leather ball filled with feathers and hair through an opening into a net fixed onto long bamboo canes. The ancient Greeks and Romans also had versions of the game. Various forms of soccer were played in medieval Europe between competing villages. It was a rowdy and often violent sport as each village's team fought over an inflated pig's stomach.

In the nineteenth century the English standardized the rules, and the modern game of soccer was born. In the twentieth century, soccer spread to every part of the globe and became the most popular sport on earth. Three billion people follow their favorite teams, and over 240 million people regularly play the game in two hundred countries. There is field soccer, indoor soccer, beach soccer and "futsal"—soccer adapted for basketball courts. Today you can play soccer barefoot on dusty pitches in Uzbekistan or before thousands of fans seated in grand stadiums in London and watched by millions more on television.

Nobody planned that soccer would become the world's most popular sport, yet it happened. Why?

Soccer is just as hard to master as other games, but at a basic level it can be easily understood and played by anyone, anywhere, anytime, with any number of participants—men and women, boys and girls, old and young, rich and poor. You can drop a round ball at the feet of a three year-old child, and she can start playing soccer immediately. Try doing that with American football or Australian Rules football. Soccer is a game that can be infinitely adjusted depending upon the circumstances, resources and people involved.

That's why it is the world's game.

Adaptive methods are just like soccer. They're simple, easy to learn, fun, contagious, adaptable, transferable and low cost.

## ONE STEP AT A TIME

Breakthroughs in the advance of the Christian movement always occur on the fringe and never at the center. So it should be no surprise that the "father" of the evangelical missionary movement was an impoverished village cobbler and part-time Baptist pastor with limited formal education. His name was William Carey (1761-1834).[1]

Carey was compelled by Christ's command to make disciples of all nations. Some churchmen believed that the command to go to the nations was given only to the original apostles and that "the heathen" had already rejected the gospel. Others taught that God in his sovereignty would save the heathen when he was ready without our help. Carey answered them with a careful survey of the world and of the history of Christian missions. He argued that Christ has a kingdom that is to be proclaimed in its power to the ends of the earth. He argued that it is the duty of all Christians to engage in the proclamation of the gospel. He challenged Protestants to commit to the Great Commission, as equally binding on them as it was on the first apostles.

In 1793 Carey and his family left for India as the first missionaries of the newly formed Baptist Missionary Society. Carey, who once described himself as a "plodder" for Christ, pioneered effective strategies one step at a time that fueled a worldwide missionary movement and changed the course of history. Devoted to India, he never left it.

Carey's brilliance is revealed in the simplicity of his mission strategy. He allowed the gospel to do its work through the spoken and written Word in the language of the people. Bible translation is hard and difficult work, but once it is completed, the Scriptures can work their influence in a new culture. In thirty years, Carey and his associates made six translations of the whole Bible, twenty-three complete New Testaments and Bible portions in ten other languages. Carey's purpose was to see local believers coming together to form a church in their culture and to take responsibility for the spread of the Christian movement. His simple methods outlived him and became the pattern for the thousands of cross-cultural missionaries who followed him.

Radically for his day, Carey saw missionary work as a five-pronged advance.

First, the gospel must be preached widely by every possible method.

Second, the preaching should be supported by the translation and distribution of the Bible in the language of the people.

Third, local churches should be established outside the control of Carey's denomination back in England.

Fourth, workers were to study the background and worldview of those who were to receive the gospel.

Fifth, local believers must be mobilized quickly to spread the gospel.

More than any other individual, Carey turned the tide of Protestant thought in favor of world missions. As reports of his work reached home, others took up the challenge of world missions. Carey had laid a foundation for the most expansive spread of the gospel the world has ever seen.

## WHY ADAPTIVE METHODS ARE IMPORTANT

*When you go to war, you need to have both toilet paper and bullets at the right place at the right time.*

TOM PETERS

Adaptive methods enable a movement to function in ways that suit its changing environment and its expansion into new fields. A movement's commitment to both its core ideology *and* to its own expansion provides the catalyst for continual learning, renewal and growth.[2] Dying institutions display the opposite characteristics— willing to sacrifice their unique identity, conservative in setting goals and unable to face the reality of their mediocre performance.

Management writer Peter Drucker tells the story of a small Indian company that bought the rights to produce a motorized bicycle. It appeared to be an ideal product for India, yet the bicycles never sold. Then the firm's owner noticed that large orders came in for just the bicycle engines. Curiosity led him to the farmers who were placing the orders. He discovered they were using the engines to drive irrigation pumps that previously were hand operated. His firm became the world's largest maker of small irrigation pumps. His pumps have revolutionized farming throughout Asia.[3]

What made this Indian entrepreneur different? He saw an opportunity when no one else could. He had a small company that was looking for opportunities and willing to take a risk on them. He was curious when unexpected orders came in for engines. He got out into the real world to understand and learn from his unexpected successes. He allowed his customers to become his teachers. When he discovered why the engines were selling, he was flexible enough to rewrite his business plan. When I think of this man, a phrase comes to mind: *determined and teachable.*

The intense religious experiences that give rise to new movements would remain fleeting unless embodied in some form of human organization. This presents every new movement with a dilemma—how to keep from extinguishing the "charismatic moment" that generates white-hot faith (the first key to a movement's vitality) while giving it sustained expression in social forms.[4] When a movement fails to define itself in organizational forms, we are left with "a loose, ill-defined set of practices and ideas spreading within a population that is never weaned of its traditional commitments."[5] This is a fad, not a movement.

Dynamic missionary movements reject the demand to choose *either* a white-hot faith *or* adaptive methods. They live in the creative tension between them. A key to the success of Pentecostalism, for example, has been its ability to bring together supernaturalism and pragmatism in a curiously compatible marriage. The most effective and sustained movements live in the tension between the chaos and creativity of spiritual enthusiasm and the stability provided by effective strategies and structures. Passion must be matched with discipline for a movement to be sustained.

The Welsh Revival of 1904-1905 was led by Evan Roberts, whose ministry was based on doing only what the Spirit told him to do. Around 100,000 people made Christian commitments during the revival, and the church worldwide was deeply influenced. Despite this, Christianity in Wales continued to gradually decline. In 1906 Roberts suffered a physical and emotional collapse. By the following year Roberts had retired from public ministry to devote the rest of his life to intercessory prayer.[6] The Welsh Revival was a passing phenomenon that was not sustained by effective strategies and biblical teaching. There was no organization and no official leadership. The spiritual energy unleashed by the revival turned in on itself and was lost or flowed into other movements.

**WHAT DO ADAPTIVE METHODS LOOK LIKE?**

Adaptive methods serve the purposes of a movement without becoming an end in themselves. Here are some examples.

*Life Transformation Groups.* The building blocks of Neil Cole's Awakening Chapels are their "Life Transformation Groups" (LTGs). Two or three people meet weekly to read Scripture, confess their sins and pray for each other. They also hold each other accountable for obeying what they've learned. The accountability questions are agreed upon, and each group decides which thirty chapters of Scripture to read each week. When the group grows to four, they form two groups.

There is no central coordination or supervision of the groups. Groups reproduce all by themselves. Neil Cole believes that if people are reading large quantities of Scripture, confessing their sins and praying together, it's hard for them to get into much trouble. LTGs are an adaptive method. They are simple, reproducible, flexible and contagious.

*The Alpha course.* I know of factory workers in China and yuppies in London who are coming to faith through the Alpha course. The course is being run around the world by thousands of churches representing all major Christian denominations. It's everywhere—152 countries, 21,000 churches, and 80 percent of the prisons in Britain. Tens of thousands of ordinary people have been trained to run the courses. Eleven million people of all ages have completed the course so far. The current rate of completion is about a million a year, and it's increasing.[7]

Alpha works because it understands the importance of relational networks. Hundreds of thousands of people whose lives have been changed by Alpha invite their friends and family to participate in future courses. Guests are more likely to come and stay because of a significant relationship. Alpha courses allow people to explore the basics of the Christian faith in a relaxed and relational setting. Once they get involved, Alpha becomes a safe place to belong before they believe. They can ask any question and say what they think, and they'll be taken seriously. Shared meals, discussion and a retreat all create community around the experience of discovery.

Alpha passes the adaptive method test. It works for its intended purpose. It can take on different forms in different contexts. It can grow and multiply while maintaining quality. It is minimalist: it doesn't need plenty of money, professional staff or infrastructure to happen.

*Bible translation.* Translating the Bible is not a simple or easy process. Of the world's 6,912 languages, 2,251 languages do not have any of the Bible translated.[8] Translations can take many years to complete and often must be accompanied by literacy programs. Yet it is still an adaptive method.

Bible translation is different depending on circumstances. Wycliffe Bible Translators' mission is to make "God's Word accessible to all people in the language of their heart." The ministry of Story-Runners sends teams into oral cultures where literacy levels are low; there they translate and spread Bible stories orally.[9] Once translated, the contagious influence of the Scriptures can spread and permeate a culture. The outcome is the spread of the gospel and the planting of an indigenous church. Bible translation combined with education for literacy is one of the most effective adaptive methods in world missions.

Due to the work of Bible translators, Christianity is by far the most culturally and linguistically diverse religion of all. African-born Yale historian Lamin Sanneh points out that "Christianity has been the impulse behind the creation of more dictionaries and grammars of the world's languages than any other force in history."[10] He argues that—contrary to popular belief, and in sharp contrast to Islam—Christianity preserves indigenous life and culture because of its emphasis on mother-tongue translation.[11]

**HOW TO RECOGNIZE AN ADAPTIVE METHOD**
Adaptive methods are recognized by their fruit. These methods are functional, responsive, simple, sustainable and resilient. Adaptive methods enable a movement to function in ways that suit its changing environment and its expansion into new fields.

Movements that drift away from their core beliefs are always at risk, but so are movements that regard the way they currently function as sacred. Every method must be evaluated against the desired outcome. That means we need to be very clear about our unchanging message and mission and clearly distinguish them from our continually changing methods. We are responsible to remain true to the gospel *and* to continually evaluate the fruitfulness and effectiveness of our methods. If we don't, self-preservation will become our mission.

When powerful organizations and movements in one era end up crippled in the next, the cause is often "the failure of success."[12] They become so convinced what they are doing is right that they stop paying attention to the world around them. They stop learning and adapting. Worse still, the informal methods that brought the initial success become formalized in inflexible and complex policies and procedures. Creativity and innovation jump ship or are made to walk the plank.

There is a cure for movements that have lost touch with a changing world. They must revisit their core beliefs and then give the young and the young at heart freedom to pioneer something new. Necessity is the mother of invention. New ideas come from fresh challenges. One of the best ways to renew an existing church is for that church to plant a church and watch what happens.

I sat in a room of about forty church leaders gathered to hear one of the crosscultural missionaries I work with talk about church planting movements in Asia. He's been in the middle of the action for over a decade. He knows how to mobilize new believers to share their faith and plant churches. This man told us that one of the key elements of a church planting movement is to ensure that every new believer has a simple way of immediately sharing their story and the gospel with friends and family.

The church leaders wanted to dissect his model of evangelism. They wanted to discuss our cultural context. They wanted to go deeper. They wanted to lead this brother into complexity and abstraction where we felt safe. He listened for a while and then asked patiently and repeatedly, "But who could you share the gospel with this week? What are you willing to *do*?" We were the ones with the theological degrees, the ministry experience and the resources. He was the one with the new believers and the new churches.

**Table 3**

| Unsustainable Church Planting Strategies | Sustainable Church Planting Strategies |
| --- | --- |
| Fully fund every church plant | Train church planters to raise funds or become tentmakers |
| Require seminary training for every church planter | Multiply trainers in the field |
| Provide a coach for every church planter | Equip established church planters to coach the next wave of church planters |
| Provide long-term subsidies for struggling church plants | Allow churches to take responsibility |
| Parent churches take responsibility for the budgeting and administration of church plants | Empower church plants to set up their own system |
| Centrally plan and coordinate where and when churches are to be planted | Expect churches and church planters to seek God, do the research, and multiply churches wherever there is a need |
| Start a church | Multiply churches |
| A denomination solely responsible to identify and recruit church planters | Every church planter trains apprentices on their team for future church plants |
| Satellite congregations dependent forever on the sending church | Satellite congregations graduate quickly to interdependence and become multiplying hubs |
| A movement held together by tight organizational systems of control | A movement held together by a common cause and relationships |

Are our methods so simple that the newest believer is employing them? That's how movements multiply disciples, groups and communities of faith. They democratize their methods and allow every follower of Jesus to participate.

Methods must be simple enough so they can be reproduced easily, rapidly and sustainably. Here are some examples of sustainable and unsustainable church planting strategies.

Centralization and standardization are the enemies of innovation. The truly great companies do not make their best moves by brilliant and complex strategic planning. What they do is "try a lot of stuff and see what works."[13] Remain true to your cause and find different ways to pursue it, then test the fruit and multiply what is effective.

There is only one gospel, and there is only one church, but they must be expressed in an endless diversity of forms. Look around you. God loves diversity. That's why I like churches of all shapes and sizes and styles. That's why I would rather see ten different approaches to reaching African refugees with the gospel than just one. Adaptive methods ensure that a movement can respond effectively to a changing environment over the long haul.

## JESUS AND ADAPTIVE METHODS

As the Word made flesh, Jesus fully entered into our world. He chose to communicate and minister in ways that matched his context and were easily picked up by his disciples. His message was profound but simple. It was readily transmitted, shaped and passed on by his disciples. Here are just a few examples of how Jesus made use of adaptive methods.

*His teaching.* No other rabbi taught like Jesus. He walked from village to village and taught men and women, large crowds and small groups, in synagogues and in open fields, in small marketplaces and in private houses.[14]

Jesus' sayings and stories were brief, pointed and pregnant with meaning. They were visual and poetic, and he told them repeatedly so that they would be easily remembered and passed on to others, which is what the disciples did as Jesus sent them out.[15]

By the end of Jesus' ministry, the content of his message was imprinted on the disciples' minds and hearts. These profound but simple sayings and stories were easily transmitted as the missionary movement advanced from person to person, group to group, and culture to culture. In two thousand years his teachings and stories have not lost their appeal or power.

*Dialogue with individuals.* Jesus' encounter with the Samaritan woman (Jn 4:1-42) shows how he adapted his message to the needs of his audience, even if it was an audience of one.[16]

Jesus was tired, hot and in need of rest from the journey. Yet he began the conversation with the woman despite the many apparent obstacles between them. She was an uneducated Samaritan woman with a questionable reputation. He was a Jewish man with enemies looking for any excuse to discredit him. Jesus was the bearer of God's revelation, yet he allowed the woman to determine the direction and form of the conversation. Jesus took her background and her responses seriously and used them as opportunities to share the gospel. He used her language in communicating his message. He also addressed her personally and dealt with the key issue in her life. He had a universal message but shaped it in a way that was meaningful to this woman. He was patient and allowed the truth of who he was to gradually dawn on her. She was important to him.

When the disciples returned, Jesus used his conversation with the woman as an opportunity to teach them how to share the gospel. It was occasions like these that Jesus modeled the skills the disciples would need when he sent them on short-term missions. Later in Acts we see how the disciples applied what Jesus taught them about ministry to individuals and different audiences.

*Leadership development.* Jesus trained his disciples in a way that was reproducible and transferable. He did not place unnecessary restrictions on who could be trained and entrusted with significant ministry. He expected faithfulness to the gospel in word and deed, but there were no artificial academic or institutional requirements for trainees. Furthermore, Jesus knew that the Holy Spirit would come and guide his followers into all truth and empower them for ministry. He did not leave a ministry manual behind with procedures and policies. He expected them to travel light in dependence on the Spirit and, just as Jesus had done, to adapt the unchanging message of the gospel to each circumstance.

Jesus did not come to found a religious organization. He came to found a missionary movement that would spread to the ends of the earth. Right from the beginning, he modeled a commitment to methods that were adaptable, transferable and readily reproducible. Then, most importantly, he left his followers to do it with the promise of his guiding presence through the Holy Spirit.

The early Christians carried out the mission entrusted to them with great courage, ingenuity and flexibility. They had no model of an international movement to work from; none had ever existed. There were no precedents. They confronted a dominant, antagonistic religious and political culture with their limited finances and organizational support. Yet the gospel went out through them from Jerusalem to Judea, Samaria and the ends of the earth. Their strategy was simple: they wanted to win as many people as possible to faith in Jesus Christ and gather them into communities that became mission centers as they eagerly awaited his return.[17]

Following the example of Jesus, Paul took his listeners seriously. He described himself as a free man who became the slave of all for the sake of the gospel. Paul adapted his methods for the sake of winning some; he was willing to be "all things to all people" (1 Cor 9:22 NRSV), whatever their background. His goal was to win people.

Paul never said he would become an adulterer to the adulterers or a pagan to the pagans. The gospel—not pragmatism—determined the limits of his flexibility as a missionary. Paul argued for cultural relevance, not cultural relativism (1 Cor 9:19-23).[18] He was under no illusion that if somehow he could get the form of the message "right" for the culture, then people would believe. He knew that the Jews expected God to reveal himself in power and glory, while the Greeks looked for wisdom. Neither of them could comprehend a God who revealed himself in the cross (1 Cor 1:22-25).[19] Despite his willingness to adapt himself to his audience, Paul taught that behind the effectiveness of the gospel is God's powerful presence through the Holy Spirit (1 Thess 1:5-6).

An important element in Paul's strategy was the establishment of new churches. He did not just win converts, he gathered them into communities of faith. Much of the ministry of Paul and his team was focused on visits and letters to the churches, the training of local leaders, and the correction of dangerous errors in belief and behavior. The churches met in homes for worship, teaching and mutual support, and were largely run by local believers. Paul's aim was to bring each new church to maturity so he could move on to the next destination, with the church as a partner in his mission.

Christianity's stubborn intransigence combined with flexibility in methods was a key to its success.[20] Early Christianity refused to compromise its essential beliefs in the struggle with paganism, and with the social and moral practices of the surrounding cultures. Stubbornness gave Christianity its internal strength, while flexibility enabled Christianity to adjust itself to the social, intellectual and cultural context. Christianity was adaptable without being syncretic.

Syncretism, the attempt to fuse the Christian faith with one or more opposing beliefs, is at its heart the denial of the uniqueness of the gospel. Christianity resisted a syncretic impulse: the Jerusalem council (Acts 15) rejected the attempt by some to impose the requirements of the Jewish law on Gentile believers; on another front the early church resisted the attempts by the Roman state and the Greek culture to make Christianity just one of a range of acceptable religions. Christianity made itself at home in both the Jewish and Greco-Roman worlds and yet did not sacrifice its message to win acceptance.

## LEARNING FROM "BARNEY"

I was visiting some of the crosscultural missionaries I work with in Asia. I was packing to go to the airport when someone mentioned there was a New Zealand couple in the city who had seen over three thousand people come to faith in a church planting movement. After a quick call, I dashed to meet "Barney" on my way to the airport.

Barney is short for Barnabas. He is in a restricted access country, and I can't tell you his real name. But the story was true. There had been thousands of people converted and hundreds of churches planted—although in a way that I did not expect.

Most of the converts had never met Barney. He was known by only a handful of leaders in the movement. In the early years he had brought some of the key leaders to Christ; immediately he concentrated on helping them to win their friends and families and to plant churches.

Many factors contributed to this amazing story of gospel advance. The aspect I want to focus on relates to adaptive methods. Barney began his ministry assuming it was his role to be the evangelist, teacher and church planter. His early efforts didn't meet with much success, so he decided to become a learner. He looked for the evidence of God's activity in the field. He watched and saw what God was blessing. He even saw God's activity in setbacks.

When Barney visited some communities, the police would arrive to find out why he was there. So he decided for security reasons to play a background role and equip new converts to do the ministry. Soon he discovered that this was not just good for security, it was also good church planting practice. The new believers could do a far better job than he could. A paradigm shift was going on in his understanding of his role and strategy.

Barney became convinced that foreigners don't make the best church planters—local believers do. He discovered he could contribute as a partner with locals through coaching, resources, problem solving and training. He made sure that everything he did was simple, effective and transferable.

Many crosscultural missionaries focus on "contextualization." They want to ensure the gospel and the church comes in a form that is relevant to the receptor culture. Barney's first concern is with "indigenization"—ensuring local believers take responsibility for the spread of the gospel. If that happens, they will do the best job of making the forms of the gospel and the church relevant to their culture.

As the leaders matured, Barney became less directly involved. Today he is partnering with them to plant churches in unreached cities, as well as training other local and foreign workers to apply the same principles. He has connected with practitioners in other locations who have been on a similar journey. For each of them these discoveries began when they confronted their lack of progress and asked, "How can we partner with what God is doing?"

In recent years these workers have pooled their learning, and exciting new strategies are bearing fruit around the world. David Garrison's book *Church Planting Movements*[21] captures this new paradigm of missions, which is really an old paradigm rediscovered.

## CONCLUSION

To fulfill their mission, the most effective movements are prepared to change everything about themselves except their basic beliefs. Unencumbered by tradition, movements feel free to experiment with new forms of the church and new effective methods of ministry. Movements embody their vision and values in systems that are effective, flexible and reproducible, outlasting and even surpassing the influence of the first generation of leaders.

Adaptive methods are the scaffolding of a movement, not the building itself. They remind us that the kingdom of heaven must be grounded in everyday practicalities. A living organism cannot survive without effective systems that can adapt to different environments. The good news of Jesus Christ is unchanging and eternal, yet its form must continually change in response to each situation. Our methods must serve our message by ensuring that the gospel can spread unhindered across cultural and geographic boundaries.

# Conclusion

## *The Future Is Already Here*

**W**e have looked at five recurring lessons on what it means for God's people to be a missionary movement. Those lessons are not a program or a formula, and their application differs in every context. So don't be concerned if you're not sure where or how to begin. The best practitioners rarely do.

Here are the stories of two leaders, one in Kenya and one in Australia. These leaders have made an impressive start, and they continue to learn what a missionary movement is all about.

### GROWING SONS AND DAUGHTERS: NAIROBI CHAPEL

I visited Africa for the first time in 2008 and met Oscar Muriu, pastor of the Nairobi Chapel in Kenya. When Oscar took over the leadership of the Nairobi Chapel in 1989, he had the advantage of not knowing what he was doing. He was twenty-seven years old and the first African pastor of a dwindling and predominantly white congregation. The church had a dream for the rebirth of Nairobi Chapel as an African congregation reaching out to the surrounding community, which included the University of Nairobi.

Oscar set about reaching university students; from the start, he focused on growing leaders rather than growing the church. He set up an internship program at no cost to the church. The interns raised their own support. Oscar made sure that each intern was presented with challenging opportunities that he hoped would keep them on their knees—or at least lying awake at night worrying.

Oscar developed the internship model by asking, "What did Jesus do with the Twelve?" He came up with five things: Jesus spent time teaching them. He put them into teams. He sent them out to do ministry. He demonstrated and taught them how to pray and apply the Scriptures to their lives. Lastly, Jesus prepared them to take responsibility when he left.

By the year 2000 Nairobi Chapel had grown to almost four thousand adults and children, and had planted seven churches. Then Oscar took his commitment to grow leaders one step further. He got his elders to agree that he was only allowed to preach half the time, and the rest of the time he had to train up others to preach. The worship leader led half of the time and trained new worship leaders for the other half. The children's teachers could only teach half the sessions and spent the rest of the time training new teachers. All elders were to mentor the people that would replace them when their second term finished.

Now Oscar had a problem. He looked out over the church and realized he had too many leaders. He knew that if they remained underutilized, they would soon become bored; eventually their frustration would come out as criticism. So Oscar divided his church of four thousand into five churches. He sent out some of his best interns in their twenties as church planters. He also sent experienced elders, most of whom were in their thirties, to support the church planters. Each church planting team went out with trained and experienced worship leaders, home group leaders, children's workers and youth workers.

The growing network of churches is now multiplying interns as each new church develops its own program. I visited Oscar in Nairobi and met one of his church planters. This man had walked away from a lucrative legal career because of the impact of the internship program on his life. Over a dinner of barbecued goat I asked him, "How many interns do you have?" "Ten," he replied. Oscar's people have mastered the difference between growth by addition and growth by multiplication.

Today Nairobi Chapel has planted twenty-five congregations in Nairobi, with thousands of members. Fourteen of the churches are in the slums of Nairobi where the members do evangelism, make disciples, grow leaders and plant churches right where the people are. By 2020 Oscar and his team want to plant three hundred churches in Kenya, other parts of Africa, Europe, Asia and America.

I asked Oscar the key to his success. He told me, "All I do is copy. You don't have to be clever to copy. I look at Scripture and ask, 'What did Jesus do?' They call that obedience."

The one statement he made that I will never forget was, "Steve, I don't plant churches. I grow sons." And some of his best "sons" are daughters; about half of his interns are women.

Oscar is a movement leader. He hasn't held onto his power and his position as the pastor of a large church. Instead he has chosen to use his position and power to serve a missionary movement and to grow leaders who do the same. Isn't that what Jesus would do?

## ADOPTING A BLOCK: BERKLEY, AUSTRALIA

Berkley is a small working-class town south of Sydney, Australia. Unemployment is high since the steel mills closed down. Some families are second- and third-generation welfare recipients who spend hours every day watching television. Wayne Pickford is a former professional wrestler who had a heart to reach out to these folks. In 2007 he staged a wrestling match to connect with the community—and to launch a church at the same time.

Wayne gathered a small team who were passionate about Jesus and had a heart for evangelism. Often these people were sidelined in existing churches because they were so zealous. Wayne took these zealots, taught them how to love people and released them to become the pastors of a neighborhood. They "adopt" one block at a time and begin knocking on doors. They visit every house, every month, with the intention of offering Jesus' love to people.

The team members go out to serve the community and to wait for opportunities to share the gospel. They've been visiting three different people with terminal-stage cancer. Most weeks it's the only visit those folks receive. There aren't enough workers to cover every neighborhood, so people ask, "When will you visit our street?" People are also signing up to join Alpha study groups that explore what it means to be a Christian. Some have volunteered to join an "adopt-a-block" team.

Wayne's qualifications for ministry are his working-class background and his experiences as a prison officer and professional wrestler. He has not graduated from seminary, and he is not ordained—but he does know how to share the gospel with people who need Jesus. He does know how to recruit a team of pioneers to go into an unreached town. He does know how to make disciples and gather them together. He does know how to help new disciples reach their friends and family with the good news.

Wayne looks across Australia and sees hundreds of towns and suburbs just like Berkley. He's already thinking about how he could train and release teams to go to those towns. His denomination is nervous because Wayne has no formal qualifications. Existing churches will get upset that Wayne and his teams come into "their" parish. If Wayne asked me what to do about these concerns, I'd ask him, "What did Jesus do? What would it look like for you to continue Jesus' ministry in the power of the Holy Spirit?"

## NEWS FROM AROUND THE WORLD

In different contexts, in different parts of the world, Oscar and Wayne are asking, "What does it look like to obey Jesus and take his command seriously to make disciples?" Their starting point is the gospel of Jesus Christ and the church as a missionary movement. In their own way, they each reveal the characteristics of dynamic movements: white-hot faith, commitment to a cause, contagious relationships, rapid mobilization and adaptive methods.

Oscar and Wayne are not alone. They are part of the global Christian movement that is changing the world. The evidence of that change is plain to see. The transformation of Christianity over the last century from a largely European faith to a truly global community has been astonishing. A century ago there were hardly any Christians in Korea. Today South Korea has 16,616 crosscultural missionaries in 173 countries; only the United States sends out more missionaries. Seoul, the South Korean capital, contains eleven of the world's twelve largest congregations.

It's not just the Koreans; the Indians, Chinese, Brazilians and Nigerians are heavily involved in reaching their own nations and in pursuing world missions. The Nigeria-based Redeemed Christian Church of God has congregations in ninety countries around the world, including America. Nigerians lead some of the largest churches in Britain. In India (which will soon surpass China as the world's most populous nation), you're not a serious player unless you've planted two thousand churches. I keep meeting movement leaders who have done just that and more. One friend has a goal of a hundred thousand churches and has made a good start. Another has a vision for a church in every one of India's one million villages and for every one of India's 4,693 people groups.

Every day over 91 percent of the global increase in the number of Christians can be found in Africa, Asia or Latin America. In the mid-twentieth century, when China came under communist rule, thousands of missionaries were forced to leave, and churches were strictly controlled or driven underground. Cut off from Western finances and training, the church in China should have collapsed. Instead it expanded beyond anyone's expectations. Today no one knows exactly how many Christians there are in China, but the estimates vary from 60 to 100 million, and the number continues to grow at a rate of 16,500 new believers every day.[1] The vast majority of these believers participate in churches that function as missionary movements with an intense commitment to reach their nation. In addition, there has been a widespread movement within the Chinese church to take the gospel west through predominantly Muslim Central Asia and the Middle East "back to Jerusalem" from where it came. The vision is to send out 100,000 Chinese missionaries, and the sending has already begun. Over the next thirty years China will continue to be the rising world economic and military power. It will also become the home to millions of new believers and a new center for the global expansion of Christianity.

Europe tells the bleaker story of a secular utopia that never materialized. Gone is a commitment to faith and family. Europe is prosperous, but its society is unsustainable. A society that has turned away from God can only find fulfillment in short-term hedonism. Islam is on the rise there, largely through a combination of immigration and the high fertility rates of Muslims already in Europe. The established churches are hopelessly secularized, rendered impotent by the legacy of state support. The Church of England cannot afford to pay the 1.4 billion British pounds required to maintain its existing buildings. Over the next decade, thousands of these churches will be forced to close.

The news out of Europe is not all bad. Europe's evangelicals, charismatics and Pentecostals continue to grow both in absolute numbers and in percentage of population. They outnumber Muslims in Europe by a ratio of two to one.[2]

As the established churches of Europe collapse, there has been significant growth in immigrant churches among Africans, Asians and Latin Americans. The growth has been in vitality as well as in numbers. The largest church in Europe is in Kiev, Ukraine. It has thirty thousand members (mostly white) and was founded by a Nigerian, Sunday Adelaja. One hundred such churches have been planted throughout the Ukraine, with two hundred such churches planted in the former Soviet Union, throughout Europe and in the rest of the world.[3] In London three of the four largest churches—all with thousands of attenders— are heavily dominated by immigrants.

In the United States a number of church multiplication networks have emerged. Tim Keller planted the Redeemer Presbyterian Church in New York, one of the most secular cities in America. The church has grown to thousands and has become a training center for church planters. Redeemer has started seventeen churches in New York; it also helped Pentecostals, Southern Baptists and Lutherans plant another fifty churches in the city. Meanwhile, city-center churches modeled on Redeemer have sprung up in places like Boston, Washington, San Francisco, Berlin, London and Amsterdam.[4]

In 1996 Mark Driscoll planted Mars Hill Church in Seattle, Washington, a city in which he says there are more dogs than Christians. The church has grown, and Mark's example has inspired others, leading Mark to form the Acts 29 network. So far, 170 Acts 29 churches have been started in America, Canada, Africa, India, Thailand and soon Australia.

Down in Texas, Bob Roberts was not content to just plant one church. Under his leadership NorthWood Church has planted fourteen churches within a radius of ten miles. You may be forgiven for thinking that anyone can plant churches in Texas, but NorthWood's church planting arm, Glocalnet, has helped to start over one hundred churches around the world, reaching thirty thousand people. Many of these churches are planting churches, making NorthWood a great-great-grandparent. Bob taught me that success is not leading a large church; success is leading a church that multiplies.[5]

Tim Keller, Bob Roberts, Mark Driscoll, Ralph Moore and Neil Cole are just a few leaders whose ministries represent a growing trend in America toward a commitment to church multiplication. Church growth, and even church planting, is seen as secondary to church multiplication. They all share a strong biblical faith, a confidence in the enabling power of the Holy Spirit, and a heart to make disciples in their backyard and around the world.

## HOW THE STORY ENDS

There are many more stories that could be told from faraway places like Mongolia and Nepal, stories of how brothers and sisters in Christ are displaying white-hot faith, commitment to the cause, contagious relationships, rapid mobilization and adaptive methods—even as you read this book. The gospel of Jesus Christ continues to spread by the grace and power of God. These movements are changing the world.

Do you want to play a part in this great cause? Imagine yourself in the upper room with the 120 people who gathered at Pentecost. Jesus has commanded you to go and make disciples of the nations. There you are with just 120 people. You do not have the resources, the knowledge or the power to get the job done.

What would it look like to align your life with Christ's command and to join a missionary movement that will one day reach every tribe, every language, every people and every nation? To be involved in seeing countless millions make Jesus Christ Lord of their lives? What needs to change in you? What do you need to do differently? Who will you go on the journey with?

One day innumerable multitudes will stand before the throne of God worshiping the Lamb that was slain. The kingdom of this world will become the kingdom of our Lord and of his Christ, and he will reign forever and ever.

This is how the drama of history will end. What part will you play?

# Study Guide

*Steve Addison,*
*Grant Morrison and*
*Buck Rogers*

**If you're a follower of Jesus,** you don't have to start a missionary movement. You're already in one. This study guide is about helping you to understand what this means and how to participate in what God is already doing.

Each study follows the main themes of *Movements That Change the World.* It would be helpful to read the relevant chapter of the book before each study. However, the focus of the lessons will not be on the content of the book but how the principles in the book are revealed in the ministry of Jesus and the early church. We've pitched these group studies at people who are ready to discover what it means to participate in a movement that is changing the world, one life at a time. If you're passionate about making disciples, this series of studies is for you.

You'll learn best if you gather with a small group of others to support and hold each other accountable as you implement the ideas. The studies can be completed over consecutive weeks or over consecutive months. What matters is that between lessons you are making a serious attempt to obey what you have learned.

# Before You Begin

**You'll need to do up to** roughly two hours of work between each session. The studies are obedience oriented; you'll be expected to put what you're learning into practice. That means following Jesus and letting him teach you how to make disciples.

There are three assignments you must complete before you can attend the first session.

1. Read through the whole of Luke-Acts and journal your observations and thoughts about the missionary movement that Jesus started.

2. Recruit a partner. Pray together and ask God to lead you to an area or a group in your region. As you sense him guide you, go and walk around the area or among the people, praying for them and making yourself open to the Holy Spirit leading you as you go. (Before you head out you may want to listen to interviews with practitioners, posted at www.movements.net as podcasts.)

3. Read "Patrick" and "Why Movements Matter" from *Movements That Change the World.*

# Why Movements Matter

## 1.1 AS YOU BEGIN . . .

Why did you decide to participate in these studies?

Discuss your time prayer walking in an area or among a people group in your region.

What do you hope will be different as a result of your involvement?

Pray together.

## 1.2 READING REVIEW

What insights did you gain from reading "Patrick" and "Why Movements Matter"?

## 1.3 MOVEMENTS THAT SHAPED OUR WORLD

Movements are made up of people committed to a common cause. They can be religious, political or social. They can be radical or conservative. Their common characteristic is that they aim to change the world. Some of the movements that have shaped the world we live in include

- Pentecostalism
- Communism
- Environmentalism
- Radical Islam
- Wikipedia

Can you think of another movement (other than Christianity) that has intersected with your life in some way? Share your experience with the group.

What are some of the characteristics of movements that change the world—for good or evil?

When you think of movements, what image or metaphor comes to mind?

A movement is like . . .

Write up the group's responses on a flip chart or large piece of paper. What do you think is hindering today's followers of Jesus from being a movement like what the metaphors represent?

## 1.4 THE MOVEMENT
## JESUS FOUNDED

Jesus founded a missionary movement that now spans the globe. The Gospels tell the story of what Jesus began to do and teach. Acts is about what Jesus continued to do through his people empowered by the Holy Spirit (Acts 1:1).

*A movement is like a river. It is constantly changing in response to new challenges yet it has one purpose—to get to the ocean.*

*The church Jesus founded was a missionary church. Its existence and activities were an expression of its missionary calling. Its members were fearlessly determined to win others to faith in Jesus as the crucified and risen Messiah. Their mission field began at home in Jerusalem and Judea, and it extended to the ends of the earth. The goal and purpose of their missionary work was the making of disciples and the creation of communities of disciples—people who turned from their old way of life, put their trust in Jesus and obeyed his teaching. (p. 30)*

From your knowledge of the Gospels and Acts, what do you think it means for followers of Jesus to be a missionary movement?

When have you experienced being part of this missionary movement?

How does your experience compare to the example of Jesus and the disciples in the Gospels and Acts?

*Missionaries establish contact with non-Christians, they proclaim the news of Jesus the Messiah and Savior (proclamation, preaching, teaching, instruction), they lead people to faith in Jesus Christ (conversion, baptism), and they integrate the new believers into the local community of the followers of Jesus (Lord's Supper, transformation of social and moral behavior, charity). (Eckhard Schnabel, quoted in* Movements That Change the World, *p. 32)*

How does this description of a missionary movement line up with what you see in Acts? Record your observations in the table below.

| Activities | Examples in Acts |
| --- | --- |
| 1. Establish contact with non-Christians. | |
| 2. Proclaim the news of Jesus as Messiah and Savior. | |
| 3. Lead people to faith in Jesus. | |
| 4. Equip disciples to form new churches. | |

## 1.5 WRAP UP

How have you been challenged by this study?

What action do you need to take before the next session to respond to this challenge?

Pray for each other.

## 1.6 BEFORE THE NEXT SESSION . . .

Luke wrote his Gospel and Acts as two parts of one story. Before your next meeting revisit Luke-Acts and the journal you wrote. Work through each of the questions in the table below.

| What to look for | What you found in Luke-Acts |
|---|---|
| What is the message that Jesus and his followers proclaimed? | |
| How is that message proclaimed? | |
| What methods and strategies are employed to spread the gospel and make disciples? | |
| How are workers selected, developed and mobilized? | |
| In what ways is the Holy Spirit at work in the ministry of Jesus and the church in Acts? | |
| How are new churches formed? | |
| How does the gospel spread into new regions and people groups? | |
| What are the barriers to the spread of the gospel, and how are they overcome? | |

# What Jesus Started

## 2.1 AS YOU BEGIN . . .

Discuss what you have been doing in response to the challenge of the last session.

## 2.2 A FRESH LOOK AT LUKE-ACTS

Refer back to the table from the last session (under 1.6). Discuss the insights into Luke-Acts that you recorded in that table.

What stirred you the most as you read Luke-Acts and the story of the expansion of the movement Jesus started? Why?

Discuss the common themes that emerged during this time of group sharing.

Which character (other than Jesus) do you most identify with in Luke-Acts? Why?

On a flip chart or large sheet of paper, brainstorm some words that describe the movement Jesus founded.

## 2.3 A FRESH LOOK AT YOUR EXPERIENCE

Fill out the table below on your current experience of church and ministry. Compare the movement that Jesus founded (see 1.6) with your current experience of church and ministry. What stands out to you?

| What to look for | Your current experience |
| --- | --- |
| What is the message we proclaim? | |
| How is that message proclaimed? | |
| What methods and strategies are employed to spread the gospel and make disciples? | |
| How are workers selected, developed and mobilized? | |
| In what ways is the Holy Spirit at work in our ministry? | |
| How are new churches formed? | |
| How does the gospel spread into new regions and people groups? | |
| What are the barriers to the spread of the gospel, and how are they overcome? | |

What would it take to bridge the gap between your current experience and what you've seen in Luke-Acts?

How will you begin to bridge that gap?

## 2.4 WRAP UP

What has challenged you from this session?

What will you do between now and the next meeting to act on what was discussed here?

Pray for each other.

## 2.5 BEFORE THE NEXT SESSION . . .

* Continue to prayer walk your area or people group. Take a partner with you. Be open to what God is saying and doing as you go.

* Read chapter one, "White-Hot Faith," from *Movements That Change the World.*

# White-Hot Faith

## 3.1 AS YOU BEGIN . . .

Take a few minutes to share how you have put into practice what you are learning about movements.

How have your prayer walks gone?

## 3.2 WHITE-HOT FAITH

Note the three best insights you gained from reading this week's chapter.

1.

2.

3.

## 3.3 YOUR STORY

Share about a time when you surrendered to God. (If your group is large, break into conversations between three or four people.)

With the whole group, talk about the lessons you learned from your experience of surrender.

> You will receive power when the Holy Spirit comes on you; and you will be my witnesses in Jerusalem, and in all Judea and Samaria, and to the ends of the earth.
>
> ACTS 1:8

## 3.4 PAUL'S CONVERSION AND CALL (ACTS 26:9-18)

*The Conversion on the Way to Damascus* is a masterpiece by Caravaggio, painted in 1601. (View the painting at <http://en.wikipedia.org/wiki/File: Caravaggio_-_La_conversione_di_ San_Paolo.jpg>.) In the painting Paul has been violently unseated from his horse. He has lost his position of power and mobility. His sword lies useless on the ground. Blinded, he stretches out his arms, pleading for help. His companion, unable to come to his aid, restrains Paul's horse from trampling him underfoot. Paul is powerless, defeated and lost. At this moment he is neither Saul nor Paul. This man has no name. He has lost everything. His life is laid bare. He is powerless to save himself.

He will arise to be led, helpless, into Damascus. After three days of blindness he will emerge as Paul the leader of a missionary movement. But at this moment he does not know this. He does not know who he is.

The great movements of the Christian faith are not human inventions. They are unleashed through the presence and power of God. Jesus brought his followers into the same wholehearted relationship he had with the Father and the Holy Spirit. He sent them to the ends of the earth with nothing but their dependence on the truth of the gospel, the reality of his power.

What is Paul surrendering to?

Imagine it is you, not Paul, who has just fallen to the ground. How do you feel?

### 3.5 THREE EXAMPLES TO FOLLOW

*Jesus.* In a surprising statement, Hebrews 5:8 tells us that, although Jesus was a son, he learned obedience from what he suffered. Jesus was the surrendered and obedient Son of the Father. The secret of his ministry was his relationship with the Father and his dependence on the power of the Holy Spirit.

How did Jesus come to the place of surrender?

How did Jesus teach his followers to surrender?

*Peter.* Peter was the outspoken disciple; however, he never suspected how low his life would get. A few hours after he declared that he would die for Jesus, he denied even knowing Jesus, three times. Later Jesus restored Peter. When the Holy Spirit came on the day of Pentecost, Peter spoke with passion and authority and launched the church as a missionary movement.

How did Peter come to the place of surrender?

What was the fruit of Peter's surrender?

*Paul.* Paul had to learn that his achievements were nothing compared to the power of knowing Christ. His troubles taught him that the gospel's power comes from God alone.

How did Paul come to the place of surrender?

What was the fruit of Paul's surrender?

What have you learned about the way God captures our hearts and empowers us for ministry?

## 3.6 WRAP UP

What is God saying to you about following Jesus in surrendering to his love and opening your life to the power of the Holy Spirit?

How will you continue to cultivate a life surrendered to God?

What will you do in response to God's call to surrender?

As you share together make sure you pray for each other.

## 3.7 BEFORE THE NEXT SESSION . . .

• Read the chapter "Commitment to a Cause."

• Continue prayer walking in your community.

• Spend some time alone with God reflecting on the passages below.

*Reflection Exercise*

Sit quietly in God's presence. Ask God to bring you to a deeper place of surrender to his love, his will and his power.

1. **Read.** Choose a passage from the list below. Read it through a number of times.

2. **Dwell.** Place yourself in the passage. For example, imagine you are one of Paul's companions on the Damascus road (Acts 9), or Peter at Pentecost (Acts 2), or Paul wresting with God about his "weakness" (2 Cor 12) or Jesus alone in the wilderness (Mt 4).

3. **Listen.** As you dwell on the passage, listen for what God is saying to you.

4. **Pray.** Let prayer well up within you in response to whatever has moved you.

Talk with Jesus about what happened for you in this time—as friend to friend.

5. **Write.** Journal your insights and write out a prayer of response to God. Repeat this exercise with the same passage if it is helpful or move on to other passages on the list.

| **Jesus**<br>Matthew 4 | **Reflections on your time of prayer** | **Your prayer of response to God** |
|---|---|---|
| **Peter**<br>Acts 2 | **Reflections on your time of prayer** | **Your prayer of response to God** |
| **Paul**<br>Acts 9<br>2 Corinthians 12 | **Reflections on your time of prayer** | **Your prayer of response to God** |

# Commitment to a Cause

## 4.1 AS YOU BEGIN . . .

Discuss highlights from your recent prayer walking.

Talk about how your time of prayer and reflection on the Scriptures went (see the table from study 3).

What response have you made to God's call to surrender?

## 4.2 COMMITMENT TO A CAUSE

Note the three best insights you gained from reading this week's chapter.

1.

2.

3.

> *Committed people make history by living in alignment with their deeply held beliefs. Missionary movements build environments that sustain and reinforce commitment to the cause. They are in*

*tension with the world around them because they have an agenda for change. They are also deeply connected with their world. It's the combination of connecting while remaining distinct that enables movements to make history. (p. 70)*

## 4.3 EXPERIENCING COMMITMENT TO A CAUSE

Share about a time when you were engaged in a cause in any sphere of life—a sporting team, a theater production, a work or community project, or a ministry assignment. What drew you to this challenge?

What did your experience teach you about being engaged in a cause?

What themes emerged as people in your group shared their stories?

Draw a picture of the moment a person becomes truly engaged in a cause.

Discuss what you've drawn with the group.

## 4.4 CONTINUING WHAT JESUS STARTED

The central figure in the book of Acts is Jesus—risen Savior and Lord. Through his Word and his Spirit, Jesus forms and grows his church. His growing band of followers play an important part in the story as they proclaim his Word in the power of the Holy Spirit.

The Gospel of Luke tells the story of what Jesus began to do. Acts tells the story of what Jesus continued to do through his followers. Today Jesus calls us to follow him and take up his cause.

*Read Luke 4:14-30.* How did Jesus model his commitment to the cause?

*Read Luke 5:1-11.* What do you notice about how Jesus calls people to his cause?

*Read Luke 10:1-8.* What would it have been like to be a member of Jesus' missionary band?

From your reading of Luke, how did Jesus ensure that his disciples clearly understood his cause and aligned their lives with it?

*Read Acts 1:1-10.* What challenge did Jesus leave with his disciples?

What resources did he provide them with?

From your reading, how did the early disciples live out their commitment to the cause entrusted to them?

What challenged their commitment?

What kept them on track?

Reread Luke 5:1-11, silently this time. Imagine Jesus has stepped into your world and called you to his cause. Write down what it would look like for you to follow him.

What would it look like for Jesus to teach you how to call others to his cause?

Share your responses with the group.

**4.5 WRAP UP**

What's one thing you need to do before you meet again?

Pray for one another.

**4.6 BEFORE THE NEXT SESSION . . .**

• Reflect on Acts 20:13-38 and 2 Timothy 4:1-8. What do they reveal about Paul's commitment to the cause? What do they say to you about aligning your life with God's purposes?

- Spend some time sitting quietly in God's presence. Ask God to bring you to a deeper place of surrender to his love, his will and his power.

- Choose a passage from the list below. Read through it a number of times. Place yourself in the passage. (For example, on the beach with Paul and the elders, or with Timothy as he reads Paul's words.)

- As you dwell on the passage listen for what God is saying to you. Let prayer well up within you in response to whatever has moved you. Talk with Jesus about what happened for you in this time—as friend to friend.

- Journal your insights and write out a prayer of response to God.

- Repeat this exercise with another passage if it is helpful.

| Paul | Reflections on Paul's commitment to the cause | Your prayer of response to God |
|---|---|---|
| Acts 20:13-38 | | |
| 2 Timothy 4:1-8 | | |

- Write a speech to your own "Ephesian elders" or a final letter to your "Timothy."

# Contagious Relationships, Part One

## 5.1 AS YOU BEGIN . . .

Share your speech or letter from section 4.6, then pray for one another.

*There is no faster or more cost effective way for an idea, a fashion, or a rumor to spread than from person to person and group to group. Technology can never replace the power of face-to-face recruitment by committed participants. Jesus understood the importance of relationships, and so did his followers.*

*It does not take vast amounts of money to fill a nation with the knowledge of the gospel. What it takes is ordinary people, on fire with the love of Christ and empowered by the Holy Spirit, who are willing to tell their families, friends and casual acquaintances what God has done for them. (p. 83)*

## 5.2 CONTAGIOUS RELATIONSHIPS

Note the three best insights you gained from reading this week's chapter.

1.

2.

3.

## 5.3 CONTAGIOUS PEOPLE

It's called the six degrees of separation. Everyone on the planet is just half a dozen handshakes away from everyone else. (See figure 3.1 on p. 80.)

*Certain people act as the links within and between social networks. Malcolm Gladwell classifies these people as connectors, mavens and salesmen. Connectors have an extraordinary ability to make multiple friends and acquaintances across different networks. With a foot in so many different relational worlds, they bring people together. Connectors are the people specialists, while mavens (Yiddish for someone who accumulates knowledge) are the information specialists—the people you go to when you need information to make a decision. They love accumulating knowledge and communicating it to others. Salesmen, meanwhile, are persuaders; they connect emotionally with others and convince them of the need to adopt new ideas or behaviors. These three types of people are the bridges over which new ideas spread contagiously from person to person and group to group. (p. 78)*

Describe someone you know who fits the description of a connector, maven or salesman.

What are some of the characteristics of contagious people? Make a list.

## 5.4 THE PERSON OF PEACE AND THE *OIKOS* (HOUSEHOLD)

As he sent out his disciples, Jesus commanded them to seek out a person of peace. This passage outlines a strategy that is still relevant today for the spread of the good news into a new field.

Read Luke 10:1-11 and describe the activities and responsibilities of the person of peace and the missionary.

> *When you enter a house, first say, "Peace to this house." If a man of peace is there, your peace will rest on him; if not, it will return to you. Stay in that house, eating and drinking whatever they give you, for the worker deserves his wages. Do not move around from house to house.*
>
> LUKE 10:5-7

| What the person of peace does | What the missionary does |
|---|---|
| | |

*Oikos* is the New Testament word for extended household or family. Every new believer has a circle of influence including family, friends, coworkers and neighbors. The person of peace is the doorway into an *oikos*.

Read the accounts of Jesus and the Samaritan woman, and of Peter and Cornelius, listed in the chart on p. 154. What do these examples teach us about how the gospel spreads to the person of peace and then to their *oikos?*

| Passage | Insights on person of peace | Insights on *oikos* |
|---|---|---|
| John 4 | | |
| Acts 10 | | |

From these passages, how did Jesus and Peter find the "person of peace"?

What obstacles were overcome to connect and communicate with these people of influence?

How is God at work in each story?

What part does the missionary play?

How did the gospel spread from an individual (person of peace) into a network of relationships (*oikos*)?

When have you seen or heard of a person of peace and an *oikos* at work?

Here are some other other passages to consider.

| Passage | Insights on person of peace | Insights on *oikos* |
|---|---|---|
| Mark 5:1-20 | | |
| John 1:1-42 | | |
| Luke 10:1-12 | | |
| Acts 16:11-15 | | |
| Acts 16:22-34 | | |

## 5.5 FINDING A PERSON OF PEACE

If you were to go looking for a person of peace, how would you begin?

Where would you go looking?

Who would you take with you?

*My wife, Michelle, suggested we go into a Chinese bookstore. I reminded her we didn't read Chinese! What was the point? Wisely I finally agreed.*

*We stepped inside and immediately met a young woman work-*

*ing in the bookstore. We chatted for a few minutes about where she was from and our visits to mainland China. Eventually we broke off the conversation and began to move on, but she would not let us go. For the next twenty minutes she followed us around the bookstore wanting to talk.*

*We'd been praying for a person of peace. I'm not sure I was confident that we would find one so quickly.*

*Eventually we got away. As we stepped outside I was overwhelmed by the experience and had to sit down. I had such a strong sense that the Holy Spirit had led us to this young woman.*

*For seven years we had lived fifteen minute's walk from thousands of unreached Chinese people, and the first time we stepped out to connect with them, God opened the door.*

*Since that time we have become good friends with the young woman. We have met many of her friends. She's a connector. Some of them have been away camping with us. We have had a number of opportunities to share Jesus with them. The story continues to unfold.*

When will you next go looking for a person of peace?


## 5.6 WRAP UP

Share your best insight from this study.


In groups of two or three, pray that God would lead you to at least one person of peace before you meet next.

## 5.7 BEFORE THE NEXT SESSION . . .

Seek out a person of peace. They may be someone you have not met before. They may be someone you meet as you prayer walk. They may be someone you already know. Remember, a person of peace is the doorway to a relational world you are not connected with.

# Contagious Relationships, Part Two

## 6.1 AS YOU BEGIN . . .

Share your experience looking for a person of peace.

Pray together for the people you connected with.

> *The most important factor [in a person's decision to adopt a new faith] is a close and positive relationship with a committed participant. (p. 77)*

Missionary movements grow exponentially when the gospel spreads through networks of preexisting relationships. For continued growth, a movement must maintain open relationships with outsiders, and it must reach out into new, adjacent social networks.

In our last study we looked at how the gospel spreads through people of peace and their networks of relationships. In this study you'll learn how to tell your story and share Jesus with others.

## 6.2 SHARING GOOD NEWS

Think of a time when you had news you couldn't wait to share with others. What was the news?

Who did you tell?


How did you tell them?


What are some reasons that we like to share and listen to stories?


What makes a story contagious—something you share?


Stories touch our emotions; stories help us connect with another person; stories are credible because they are from our own lives. In the last session we looked at how the gospel spreads via people of peace and their relational networks. As you connect with responsive people it is important that you can share your story with them simply and briefly. As you make disciples you will need to teach them to do the same.

## 6.3 PAUL'S STORY

In Acts, Paul tells his story of conversion three times (Acts 9:1-22; 22:1-21; 26:1-23).

List the main points of Paul's story from the account in Acts 9:1-22.

- Paul's life before he met Jesus (vv. 1-2):


- How he met Jesus (vv. 3-19):

- How his life changed (vv. 20-22):

## 6.4 YOUR STORY

Write down a few points under each heading.

- Your life before you met Jesus:

- How you met Jesus:

- How your life has changed:

Break into pairs and practice telling your story in these three parts. Each person has just five minutes to share his or her story. You may need to appoint a timekeeper!

*Keep practicing until you can share your story at any time with anyone. Practice telling each part using simple words that others can understand. You should be able to tell each part clearly and quickly.*

*Write up your story and bring it to the next session to share. The entire story should last about three minutes.*

## 6.5 SHARING HIS STORY

Paul in Galatians 1:8 condemns anyone who preaches another gospel than the one he declares. He takes pains to show that the gospel he declares is the same as that preached by Peter, John and the others. "Whether, then, it was I or they," Paul says, "this is what we preach, and this is what you believed" (1 Cor 15:11). Together with your own story, you

> For what I received I passed on to you as of first importance: that Christ died for our sins according to the Scriptures, that he was buried, that he was raised on the third day according to the Scriptures.
>
> 1 CORINTHIANS 15:3-4

need to be able to tell others the message of the gospel simply and briefly. This next section is to help you find a consistent way to tell the gospel.

Acts provides us with a number of different presentations of the one gospel. Read Paul's presentation in Acts 17:22-31. What are his main points?

Certain themes recur in the various gospel presentations in Acts:

*God (the nature and character of the God we proclaim)*

*Sin (which every person is guilty of and which results in death and a broken relationship with God)*

*Jesus (the only way and the returning judge; his life, death and resurrection brings forgiveness of sins)*

*Response (repentance and belief)*

*Salvation (forgiveness of sin and the gift of the Holy Spirit)*

Write down the essential truths that a person needs to understand in order to come to saving faith in Jesus Christ. Include some key Scriptures that support these essentials.

In pairs take 3-5 minutes to each share your gospel outline.

As a group, list the essentials and supporting Scriptures everyone came up with. Is anything missing?

Can anything be eliminated while still maintaining the essence of the gospel message?

It is important for new believers to start sharing their story and his story right away. That means having a simple method of sharing the gospel. There are a number of gospel presentations in appendix one.

### 6.6 WRAP UP

On your own, list the names of three people you could share your story and/or his story with before the next session.

In groups of two or three, pray for each person by name.

### 6.7 BEFORE THE NEXT SESSION . . .

• Write out your story so you can share it in three minutes.

• Master your gospel presentation or one of the presentations in appendix one and come prepared to share it in the next session.

• Share your story and/or his story with three people.

# Rapid Mobilization

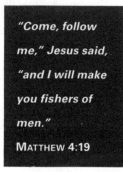

*"Come, follow me," Jesus said, "and I will make you fishers of men."*

MATTHEW 4:19

## 7.1 AS YOU BEGIN . . .

Discuss your progress in sharing your story and/or his story.

Pray for the people you shared with and any people of peace you have encountered.

In pairs practice sharing your story and your gospel presentation.

## 7.2 RAPID MOBILIZATION

Note three insights you gained from reading this week's chapter.

1.

2.

3.

*At the beginning of his ministry, Jesus recruited disciples with the promise that he would teach them how to catch people rather than fish. He refused to entrust himself to the crowds, but he entrusted himself to his disciples. Jesus reached the multitudes, but his purpose was to grow the leaders who would continue his ministry in the power of the Holy Spirit. (pp. 94-95)*

## 7.3 WORKERS FOR THE HARVEST

In the Gospels and Acts, Jesus and his disciples are often on the move. The Christian movement spread rapidly because they mobilized ordinary people for ministry.

Read Matthew 9:35-38; 10:1-15. What strikes you about how Jesus mobilized workers?

> *When they saw the courage of Peter and John and realized that they were unschooled, ordinary men, they were astonished and they took note that these men had been with Jesus.*
>
> ACTS 4:13

Read John 4:1-42. How did Jesus mobilize the Samaritan woman? How much time did it take? What qualified her for the task?

How do Jesus' methods of growing leaders differ from your experience?

## 7.4 PARTNERS IN MINISTRY

There are around one hundred names in Acts and the Epistles of different people associated with Paul in ministry. Read Romans 16:3-16 and list together the names of the people Paul identifies as coworkers—and how he describes them.

Read 2 Timothy 2:2. How many generations of workers does Paul identify?

How many generations of workers can you identify in your ministry?

Who has invested in you?

Who are you equipping?

Who are they investing in?

What do you need to do differently so that you can more rapidly mobilize workers?

## 7.5 WRAP UP

Share an important insight you have gained about rapid mobilization.

## 7.6 BEFORE NEXT THE SESSION . . .

- Seek to share your story and/or his story with a person of peace.

- Find someone (or a small group) who is willing to let you teach them about the "person of peace" and their *oikos* (relational network). Teach them how to share their story and his story.

  As they begin looking for people of peace and sharing Christ, be prepared to help them train others also.

# Adaptive Methods

## 8.1 AS YOU BEGIN . . .

Share your progress in looking for people of peace, sharing your story and sharing his story.

Pray for the people you have connected with.

## 8.2 ADAPTIVE METHODS

What are three insights you gained from reading this week's chapter?

1.

2.

3.

## 8.3 JAMES NAISMITH—INVENTOR OF BASKETBALL

*In the late 1800s James Naismith became convinced that he stood a better chance of exemplifying the Christian life through sports rather than through preaching. So he took a job as a physical education instructor at the YMCA's International Training School for Christian Workers in Springfield, Massachusetts. Naismith's vision was "to win men for the Master through the gym."*

*Naismith set out to create an indoor activity for students during the winter months. Having studied European gymnastics models, and toyed with indoor versions of football, soccer and lacrosse, Naismith spent two weeks testing various games with his athletics class—with no success. Finally, Naismith decided to draw from all of these sports: with a ball that could be easily handled, play that involved running and passing with no tackling and a goal at each end of the floor. Thus, at a Springfield YMCA in 1891, was the game of basketball born.*

*Basketball served as an important evangelical tool for many during its first 50 years. In his 1941 book "Basketball: Its Origin and Development," Naismith wrote, "Whenever I witness games in a church league, I feel that my vision, almost half a century ago, of the time when the Christian people would recognize the true value of athletics, has become a reality."*

*Amazingly, Naismith never profited from the sport he invented.*

*(John Murray, "The Spiritual Pathway to March Madness,"* Wall Street Journal, *March 18, 2010)*

Why do you think James Naismith was so effective in his attempt to create this new sport?

How is basketball an example of an adaptive method?

## 8.4 WHAT EFFECTIVENESS LOOKS LIKE

To fulfill their mission, the most effective movements are prepared to change everything about themselves except their core beliefs. Unencumbered by tradition, movements feel free to experiment with new forms and strategies. Movements pursue their mission with methods that are effective, flexible and reproducing.

As the Word made flesh, Jesus fully entered into our world. He chose to communicate and minister in ways that matched his context and were easily picked up by his disciples. His message was profound but simple. It was readily transmitted, shaped and passed on by his disciples.

| Adaptive methods | Description |
|---|---|
| Sustainable | Able to reproduce without external funding |
| Flexible | Can be modified as the context changes |
| Transferable | Easily passed on to new disciples |
| Simple | Only the essentials are included |
| Functional | Effective for the purpose they were intended |
| Scaleable | Capable of multiplying without distortion |
| Reproducing | Spreads rapidly from person to person, network to network |

## 8.5 THE MINISTRY OF JESUS

Read Luke 10:1-12. What does this passage tell you about Jesus' methods?

In what sense were they effective?

## 8.6 THE MINISTRY OF JESUS THROUGH YOU

Assess your current ministry in sharing the gospel and making disciples.

Rate your effectiveness on the continuums below.

*Sustainable*
Not effective ————————————————————— Very effective

*Flexible*
Not effective ————————————————————— Very effective

*Transferable*
Not effective ————————————————————— Very effective

*Simple*
Not effective ————————————————————— Very effective

*Functional*
Not effective ————————————————————— Very effective

*Scaleable*
Not effective ————————————————————— Very effective

*Reproducing*
Not effective ————————————————————— Very effective

As you reflect on how you make disciples, what do you need to change to be more effective?

As a whole group share how each one can become more effective in ministry methods.

## 8.7 WRAP UP

Jesus called his disciples to follow him, and he promised to teach them how to win others and make disciples. We are not alone in this challenge. Jesus is our teacher, and by his Word and his Spirit he will empower us to minister effectively.

Pray for one another's discipleship and ministry.

## 8.8 BEFORE THE NEXT SESSION . . .

- If you have found a person of peace, seek out an opportunity to share your story and/or the gospel with him or her this week. If not, keep looking and praying that God would lead you to someone.

- Go back over your notes for each of the sessions. Identify a key insight from each one.

| Session | One Key Insight |
|---|---|
| Why movements matter | |
| What Jesus started | |
| White-hot faith | |
| Commitment to a cause | |
| Contagious relationships (I) | |
| Contagious relationships (2) | |
| Rapid mobilization | |
| Adaptive methods | |

# Bringing It Together

## 9.1 AS YOU BEGIN . . .

Share how you have done sharing the gospel and looking for people of peace since you joined the group.

Pray as a group for the people you have connected with.

## 9.2 LOOKING BACK

As a group, share your key insights from each of the previous sessions (see table, session 8).

## 9.3 REFLECTION

Take ten minutes alone to answer the questions below.

1. Through these studies what have you learned about yourself?


2. What have you learned about God and how he works?


3. What will you do next?

4. On a scale of 1-10, how likely is it that you will follow through? Why?

5. What will it take to get closer to a "10"?

Discuss your responses together.

### 9.4 WHAT WILL YOU DO?

List the three most important things you need to do to implement what you have learned from these studies.
1.
2.
3.

### 9.5 PRAYER

Each person in the group share what they are going to do, then have two people pray for them.

### 9.6 WHAT'S NEXT?

The next series of studies to be developed at <www.movements.net> will deal with the components of a plan to multiply disciples and churches.
1. Reproducing ENTRY Strategy.

   How do you start talking to people about spiritual matters or take the gospel into new areas?
2. Reproducing GOSPEL Presentation.

   How will the gospel be presented?

> Jesus said, "This is what the kingdom of God is like. A man scatters seed on the ground. Night and day, whether he sleeps or gets up, the seed sprouts and grows, though he does not know how. All by itself the soil produces grain—first the stalk, then the head, then the full kernel in the head. As soon as the grain is ripe, he puts the sickle to it, because the harvest has come."
>
> MARK 4:26-29

3. Reproducing DISCIPLESHIP.

    a. Reproducing beginning/short-term discipleship (6-8 lessons)

    b. Reproducing long-term discipleship (may take 1-3 years)

4. Reproducing CHURCH Formation.

    Teaching and helping groups become church.

5. Reproducing LEADERSHIP training.

    Multiplying workers who can equip others in 1-5.

Visit us online at <www.movements.net> to provide your input and to receive news about the next series of studies.

# Gospel Presentations

A gospel presentation includes "the basics of the good news of the Lordship of Jesus Christ, his kingdom come/coming, his death, burial and resurrection, and the free forgiveness of sins for those who repent and trust in the person of Jesus Christ" (<www.theope dia.com/Gospel_presentations>; see this site for a variety of presentations). Below are some examples of concise gospel presentations in the New Testament, as well as contemporary ways of presenting the gospel.

## GETTING STARTED

1. Ask: "If it is possible to know God personally, would you like to know how?"

2. Share your story in three to five minutes.

3. Ask: "Could I show you from the Bible how you can know God personally?"

4. Share a simple gospel presentation.

### A. Two Ways to Live

1. God the creator; humanity ruling under his authority.

2. Humanity rebels, wishing to run things its own way.

3. God judges (and will judge) humanity for this rebellion.

4. In his love, God sends Jesus to die as an atoning sacrifice.

5. In his power, God raises Jesus to life as ruler and judge.

6. This presents us with a challenge to repent and believe.

<www.matthiasmedia.com.au/2wtl>

*B. How to Know God Personally*

1. God loves you and offers a wonderful plan for your life.

2. All of us sin, and our sin has separated us from God.

3. Jesus Christ is God's only provision for our sin. Through him we can know and experience God's love and plan for our life.

4. We must individually receive Jesus Christ as Savior and Lord; then we can know and experience God's love and plan for our lives.

<www.ccci.org/wij/index.aspx>

*C. Share Jesus Without Fear*

Begin by asking your friend questions about his or her beliefs. Then open your Bible and let God's Word speak for itself.

1. "For all have sinned and fall short of the glory of God" (Rom 3:23).

2. "For the wages of sin is death, but the gift of God is eternal life in Christ Jesus our Lord" (Rom 6:23).

3. "I tell you the truth, no one can see the kingdom of God unless he is born again" (Jn 3:3).

4. "I [Jesus] am the way and the truth and the life. No one comes to the Father except through me" (Jn 14:6).

5. "If you confess with your mouth, 'Jesus is Lord,' and believe in your heart that God raised him from the dead, you will be saved. For it is with your heart that you believe and are justified, and it is with your mouth that you confess and are saved. As the Scripture says, 'Anyone who trusts in him will never be put to shame'" (Rom 10:9-11).

6. "And he died for all, that those who live should no longer live for themselves but for him who died for them and was raised again" (2 Cor 5:15).

7. "Here I am! I stand at the door and knock. If anyone hears my voice and opens the door, I will come in and eat with him, and he with me" (Rev 3:20).

Take your friend through all these verses one by one, inviting him or her to read each verse aloud and explain it to you. If your friend interprets a passage incorrectly, don't argue or offer your interpretation, but politely ask him to read it again, and then explain your take on it a second time. Even if your friend mentions that he doesn't believe in or agree with the Bible, it is best not to argue. You can state that you simply want him to understand what the Bible says about eternity. <www.allaboutgod.com/share-jesus-without-fear.htm>

### D. The Bridge to Life

#### 1. God's Love
God created us in his own image to be his friend and to experience a full life assured of his love. But he didn't make us robots—he gave us the freedom of choice.

#### 2. Humanity's Problem
Humanity has chosen to disobey God and thus become separated from him. This separation means the penalty of an eternal spiritual death.

#### 3. God's Remedy
On our own, we cannot attain the perfection needed to bridge the gap between humanity and God. Christ's death alone is adequate for our sin and bridges the gulf between God and humanity.

#### 4. Our Response
Believing means trust and commitment—acknowledging our sinfulness, trusting Christ's forgiveness and letting him control our life. Eternal life is a gift for us to receive.

<http://www.ibcberlin.org/blog/wp-content/uploads/bridge.pdf>

■ ■ ■

Remember it is important that the gospel presentation you use is simple and memorable so that you can quickly train new believers to share it with their friends and family.

# Discovery Bible Study

This is a simple approach to Bible study that you can use with a person of peace and their *oikos*. From the beginning your intention should be to reproduce the group; the group must not be dependent on your input.

### 1. OPEN

What are you thankful for?

What are your needs? What are the needs of your friends and neighbors?

*As participants come to faith, the questions above can lead to prayer.*

Can this group do anything to meet those needs?

*Avoid fixing problems. This is a chance for participants to learn how God can meet needs and to be discipled for ministry.*

## 2. REVIEW

Who can retell last week's lesson?

*Ask the group to help each other remember correctly. If they get it wrong and are not corrected by the group, ask them to read the part that states what they are saying.*

Did anybody apply what they learned last week? What did you do differently because of the study?

Who did you share with and what was their reaction?

*This is important: they must learn to share with others. As they share, they need to look for responsive people rather than convince those who are not interested.*

## 3. READ

*Assign a passage from the Bible. Focus is on Scripture, not human opinion.*

## 4. DISCUSS

How would you repeat this in your own words?

What does this teach us about God?

What does this teach us about people?

If this story is true, what would you need to obey?

Who are you going to tell about what you have learned?

This approach was developed by David Watson. A detailed manual, *Discovering God*, is available on his website: <www.cpmtr.org/resources>.

# Recommended Reading
# on Movements

## BIBLICAL/MISSIOLOGICAL

Allen, Roland. *Missionary Methods: St. Paul's Or Ours?* 4th ed. London: World Dominion Press, 1912.

———. *The Spontaneous Expansion of the Church: And the Causes That Hinder It.* London: World Dominion Press, 1927.

Hooft, W. A. Visser 't. *The Renewal of the Church: The Dale Lectures.* Delivered at Mansfield College, Oxford, October 1955. London, SCM Press, 1956.

Schnabel, Eckhard J. *Early Christian Mission,* vol. 1, *Jesus and the Twelve.* Downers Grove, Ill.: IVP Academic, 2004.

———. *Early Christian Mission,* vol. 2, *Paul and the Early Church.* Downers Grove, Ill.: IVP Academic, 2004.

———. *Paul the Missionary: Realities, Strategies and Methods.* Downers Grove, Ill.: IVP Academic, 2008.

Winter, Ralph D. *The Unfolding Drama of the Christian Movement.* Pasadena, Calif.: Institute of International Studies, 1979.

Winter, Ralph, and Steven Hawthorne. *Perspectives on the World Christian Movement: A Reader.* Milton Keynes, U.K.: Paternoster Press, 2009.

## HISTORICAL

Anderson, Allan. *Spreading Fires: The Missionary Nature of Early Pentecostalism.* Maryknoll, N.Y.: Orbis, 2007.

Cahill, Thomas. *How the Irish Saved Civilization: The Untold Story of Ireland's Heroic Role From the Fall of Rome to the Rise of Medieval Europe.* New York: Doubleday, 1995.

Heitzenrater, Richard P. *Wesley and the People Called Methodists*. Nashville: Abingdon, 1994.

Hutton, J. E. *A History of the Moravian Church*. 2nd ed. London: Moravian Publication Office, 1909.

Lewis, Arthur James. *Zinzendorf, the Ecumenical Pioneer: A Study in the Moravian Contribution to Christian Mission and Unity*. Philadelphia: Westminster Press, 1962.

Pierson, Paul E. *The Dynamics of Christian Mission: History Through a Missiological Perspective*. Pasadena, Calif.: William Carey International University Press, 2008.

Pollock, John Charles. *A Cambridge Movement*. London: John Murray, 1953.

Snyder, Howard A. *Signs of the Spirit: How God Reshapes the Church*. Grand Rapids: Academie Books, 1989.

## SOCIOLOGICAL

Finke, Roger. "Innovative Returns to Tradition: Using Core Teachings as the Foundation for Innovative Accommodation." *Journal for the Scientific Study of Religion* 43, no. 1 (2004): 19-34.

Finke, Roger, and Rodney Stark. *The Churching of America, 1776-1990: Winners and Losers in Our Religious Economy*. New Brunswick, N.J.: Rutgers University Press, 1992.

Gerlach, Luther P., and Virgina H. Hine. *People, Power, Change: Movements of Social Transformation*. Indianapolis: Bobbs-Merrill, 1970.

Kelley, Dean M. *Why Conservative Churches Are Growing: A Study in Sociology of Religion*. San Francisco: HarperCollins, 1972.

Kuhn, Thomas S. *The Structure of Scientific Revolutions*. 2nd ed. Chicago: University of Chicago Press, 1970.

Stark, Rodney. *The Rise of Christianity: A Sociologist Reconsiders History*. Princeton, N.J.: Princeton University Press, 1996.

———. *Cities of God: The Real Story of How Christianity Became an Urban Movement and Conquered Rome*. San Francisco: HarperSanFrancisco, 2006.

## ORGANIZATIONAL

Adizes, Ichak. *Corporate Lifecycles: How and Why Corporations Grow and Die and What to Do About It*. 4th ed. Englewood Cliffs, N.J.: Prentice Hall, 1998.

———. *Managing Corporate Lifecycles*. Paramus, N.J.: Prentice Hall, 1999.

Barabasi, Albert-Laszlo. *Linked: How Everything Is Connected to Everything Else and What It Means*. New York: Plume, 2003.

Brafman, Ori, and Rod A. Beckstrom. *The Starfish and the Spider: The Unstop-*

*pable Power of Leaderless Organizations.* New York: Portfolio, 2006.

Collins, Jim. *Good to Great: Why Some Companies Make the Leap . . . and Others Don't.* New York: Harper Collins, 2001.

————. *Good to Great and the Social Sectors: A Monograph to Accompany Good to Great.* London: Random House, 2006.

Collins, Jim, and Jerry I. Porras. *Built to Last: Successful Habits of Visionary Companies.* London: Century, 1994.

Godin, Seth. *Tribes: We Need You to Lead Us.* New York: Penguin, 2008.

## CONTEMPORARY

Cole, Neil. *Organic Church: Growing Faith Where Life Happens.* San Francisco: Jossey-Bass, 2005.

Garrison, David. *Church Planting Movements: How God Is Redeeming a Lost World.* Midlothian, Va.: WIGTake Resources, 2004.

Gupta, Paul R., and Sherwood G. Lingenfelter. *Breaking Tradition to Accomplish Vision: Training Leaders for a Church-Planting Movement: A Case from India.* Winona Lake, Ind.: BMH Books, 2006.

Hirsch, Alan. *The Forgotten Ways: Reactivating the Missional Church.* Grand Rapids: Brazos Press, 2007.

Jenkins, Philip. *The Next Christendom: The Coming of Global Christianity.* New York: Oxford University Press, 2002.

Logan, Robert E. *Be Fruitful and Multiply.* Carol Stream, Ill.: Churchsmart Resources, 2006.

McClung, Floyd. *You See Bones, I See an Army: Changing the Way We Do Church.* Eastbourne, U.K.: David C. Cook, 2007.

Moore, Ralph. *How to Multiply Your Church: The Most Effective Way to Grow.* Ventura, Calif.: Gospel Light, 2009.

Roberts, Bob, Jr. *The Multiplying Church: The New Math for Starting New Churches.* Grand Rapids: Zondervan, 2008.

Schwarz, Christian A. *Color Your World with Natural Church Development: Experiencing All That God Has Designed You to Be.* Carol Stream, Ill.: Churchsmart Resources, 2005.

# Notes

## PATRICK

[1]See Philip Freeman, *St. Patrick of Ireland: A Biography* (New York: Simon & Schuster, 2005), p. xi.

[2]Patrick, *Confessions,* Catholic Information Network, 1996, accessed March 15, 2009 at <www.cin.org/patrick.html>.

[3]Philip Jenkins has written an excellent account of the spread of Christianity in the Middle East, Africa and Asia. Christianity did spread beyond the borders of the Roman Empire; yet this was in spite of the lack of missionary zeal within the empire, not because of it. See Philip Jenkins, *The Lost History of Christianity: The Thousand-Year Golden Age of the Church in the Middle East, Africa and Asia—and How It Died* (New York: HarperOne, 2008).

[4]Freeman, *St. Patrick of Ireland,* p. 75.

[5]Thomas Cahill, *How the Irish Saved Civilization: The Untold Story of Ireland's Heroic Role from the Fall of Rome to the Rise of Medieval Europe* (New York: Doubleday, 1995), p. 128.

[6]Kathleen Hughes questions if Patrick's position as missionary bishop was ever officially sanctioned. He begins his letter to Coroticus: "[I] declare myself to be a bishop. Most assuredly I believe that what I am I have received from God." See Kathleen Hughes, *The Church in Early Irish Society* (Ithaca, N.Y.: Cornell University Press, 1966), pp. 34-35.

[7]Freeman, *St. Patrick of Ireland,* p. 141.

[8]See Stephen Neill, *A History of Christian Missions,* Pelican History of the Church (Harmondsworth, U.K.: Penguin, 1964), p. 57.

[9]Freeman, *St. Patrick of Ireland,* p. 82.

[10]John T. McNeill, *The Celtic Churches: A History A.D. 200 to 1200* (Chicago: University of Chicago Press, 1974), pp. 70, 80.

[11]Richard Fletcher, *The Conversion of Europe: From Paganism to Christianity, 371-1386 A.D.* (London: Fontana, 1997), p. 91.

[12]See Kenneth Scott Latourette, *A History of Christianity*, vol. 1, *Beginnings to 1500*, rev. ed., with foreword and supplemental bibliographies by Ralph D. Winter (New York: Harper and Row, 1975), p. 102.

[13]See McNeill, *Celtic Churches*, pp. 192, 224.

[14]McNeill comments, "Complete freedom from superiors beyond their own communities in the mission field made them adaptable to local needs and opportunities. They rapidly enlisted Frankish and other German youth who, working harmoniously with them, made Christianity indigenous and self-perpetuating." McNeill, *Celtic Churches*, p. 175; see also pp. 155-56 for autonomy on the mission field.

[15]Cahill, *How the Irish Saved Civilization*, p. 155.

[16]Ibid., pp. 194-96. See also McNeill, *Celtic Churches*, p. 155; and Kenneth Scott Latourette, *A History of the Expansion of Christianity*, vol. 1, *The First Five Centuries* (London: Eyre and Spottiswoode, 1938), p. 38.

## INTRODUCTION: WHY MOVEMENTS MATTER

[1]*Dilaram* is a Farsi/Persian word for *peace*. Floyd tells the story of Dilaram in Floyd McClung, *Living on the Devil's Doorstep: From Kabul to Amsterdam* (Seattle: YWAM Publishing, 1999).

[2]See Eckhard J. Schnabel, *Early Christian Mission*, vol. 1, *Jesus and the Twelve* (Downers Grove, Ill.: IVP Academic, 2004), p. 95.

[3]See Matthew 12:46-50 and Schnabel, *Early Christian Mission*, 1:355-56.

[4]I. Howard Marshall, *New Testament Theology: Many Witnesses, One Gospel* (Downers Grove, Ill.: InterVarsity Press, 2004), pp. 34-37, 709-10.

[5]Alan Hirsch, *The Forgotten Ways: Reactivating the Missional Church* (Grand Rapids: Brazos Press, 2007), p. 82.

[6]Following Schnabel, *Early Christian Mission*, 1:11-12.

[7]Eckhard J. Schnabel, *Paul the Missionary: Realities, Strategies and Methods* (Downers Grove, Ill.: IVP Academic, 2008), p. 29.

[8]*Founding charism* is a term used by Catholic religious orders to describe the gift given to a person or group to understand and live out, with intensity, an aspect of the gospel.

[9]Kenneth Scott Latourette, *A History of the Expansion of Christianity*, vol. 4, *The Great Century in Europe and the United States of America A.D. 1800-A.D. 1914* (London: Eyre and Spottiswoode, 1941), pp. 22, 26.

[10]Paul E. Pierson, lecture notes, "Historical Development of the Christian

Movement" (Pasadena, Calif.: Fuller School of World Mission, 1988).
[11]See 1 Corinthians 1:18-2:5 and Schnabel, *Paul the Missionary*, pp. 356-82.

## CHAPTER 1: WHITE-HOT FAITH

[1]For the importance of Word, Spirit and mission held together in synthesis see Stuart Piggin, *Spirit of a Nation: The Story of Australia's Christian Heritage* (Sydney: Strand, 2004), p. v.

[2]Colin A. Grant, "Europe's Moravians: A Pioneer Missionary Church," in *Perspectives on the World Christian Movement: A Reader*, ed. Ralph D. Winter and Steven C. Hawthorne (Pasadena, Calif.: William Carey Library, 1999), p. 276.

[3]See Arthur James Lewis, *Zinzendorf, the Ecumenical Pioneer: A Study in the Moravian Contribution to Christian Mission and Unity* (Philadelphia: Westminster Press, 1962), p. 92.

[4]Stephen Neill, *A History of Christian Missions* (Harmondsworth, U.K.: Penguin Books, 1964), p. 237; and Kenneth Scott Latourette, *A History of the Expansion of Christianity*, vol. 3, *Three Centuries of Advance* (London: Eyre and Spottiswoode, 1938), pp. 47-48.

[5]Howard A. Snyder, *Signs of the Spirit: How God Reshapes the Church* (Grand Rapids: Academie Books, 1989), p. 154.

[6]Lewis, *Zinzendorf, the Ecumenical Pioneer*, p. 73.

[7]Vinson Synan, *The Holiness-Pentecostal Tradition: Charismatic Movements in the Twentieth Century* (Grand Rapids: Eerdmans, 1997), p. 99.

[8]Grant McClung, "Pentecostals: The Sequel," *Christianity Today*, April 2006, p. 29.

[9]Philip Jenkins, *The Next Christendom: The Coming of Global Christianity* (New York: Oxford University Press, 2002), p. 2.

[10]For examples see Elizabeth E. Brusco, *The Reformation of Machismo: Evangelical Conversion and Gender in Columbia* (Austin: University of Texas Press, 1995); and Donald E. Miller and Tetsunao Yamamori, *Global Pentecostalism: The New Face of Christian Social Engagement* (Berkeley: University of California Press, 2007).

[11]See Joachim Jeremias, *New Testament Theology: The Proclamation of Jesus* (London: SCM Press, 1971), 1:64-66.

[12]See Eckhard J. Schnabel, *Early Christian Mission*, vol. 1, *Jesus and the Twelve* (Downers Grove, Ill.: IVP Academic, 2004), p. 273.

[13]See Jenkins, *Next Christendom*.

[14]Lamin Sanneh, *Whose Religion Is Christianity? The Gospel Beyond the West* (Grand Rapids: Eerdmans, 2003), pp. 14-15.

[15]Jenkins, *Next Christendom*, p. 123.

[16]Martin Robinson, *Planting Mission-Shaped Churches Today* (Oxford: Monarch Books, 2006), p. 144.

**CHAPTER 2: COMMITMENT TO A CAUSE**

[1]Victor Hugo, *Histoire d'un Crime* (History of a Crime) (written 1852, published 1877); accessed May 26, 2009, at <http://en.wikiversity.org/wiki/Victor_Hugo_quote>.

[2]Parker J. Palmer, *Let Your Life Speak: Listening to the Voice of Your Vocation* (San Francisco: Jossey-Bass, 2000), p. 32.

[3]See Dean M. Kelley, *Why Conservative Churches Are Growing: A Study in Sociology of Religion* (San Francisco: HarperCollins, 1972).

[4]John Wesley, *The Journal of John Wesley*, January 13, 1738; accessed March 24, 2004, at <www.ccel.org/ccel/wesley/journal.html>.

[5]Ibid., May 24, 1738.

[6]John Wesley, "Minutes of Several Conversations Between Rev. John Wesley, A.M., and the Preachers in Connexion With Him," question 3; accessed March 29, 2009, at <www.archive.org/stream/minutesofseveral00wesliala/minutesofseveral00wesliala_djvu.txt>.

[7]John Wesley, quoted in George G. Hunter, *To Spread the Power: Church Growth in the Wesleyan Spirit* (Nashville: Abingdon, 1987), p. 58.

[8]Howard A. Snyder, *The Radical Wesley and Patterns for Church Renewal* (Downers Grove, Ill.: InterVarsity Press, 1980), p. 54.

[9]Ibid., p. 225.

[10]Wesley, *Journal*, August 2, 1763.

[11]Snyder, *Radical Wesley*, p. 230.

[12]See Stephen Tomkins, *John Wesley: A Biography* (Grand Rapids: Eerdmans, 2003).

[13]Kelley, *Why Conservative Churches Are Growing*, p. 119.

[14]See Margaret J. Wheatley, *Leadership and the New Science: Learning About Organization from an Orderly Universe* (San Francisco: Berrett-Koehler, 1992), pp. 18-19.

[15]See Lawrence Cada, Raymond Fitz, Gertrude Foley, Thomas Giardino and Carol Lichtenberg, *Shaping the Coming Age of Religious Life* (New York: Seabury Press, 1979).

[16]See Roger Finke, "Innovative Returns to Tradition: Using Core Teachings as the Foundation for Innovative Accommodation," *Journal for the Scientific Study of Religion* 43, no. 1 (March 2004): 19-34.

[17]See Rosabeth Moss Kanter, *Commitment and Community: Communes and Utopias in Sociological Perspective* (Cambridge, Mass.: Harvard University Press, 1972).

[18]Jim Collins and Jerry I. Porras, *Built to Last: Successful Habits of Visionary Companies* (London: Century, 1994), pp. 138-39.

[19]See Laurence R. Iannaccone, "Why Strict Churches Are Strong," *American Journal of Sociology* 99 (1994): 1180-1211.

[20]Rodney Stark, "How New Religions Succeed," in *The Future of New Religious Movements*, ed. David G. Bromley and Phillip E. Hammond (Mercer, Ga.: Mercer University Press, 1987), pp. 15-16.

[21]Christian Smith, *American Evangelicalism: Embattled and Thriving* (Chicago: University of Chicago Press, 1998), p. 10.

[22]See I. Howard Marshall, *New Testament Theology: Many Witnesses, One Gospel* (Downers Grove, Ill.: InterVarsity Press, 2004), pp. 184-206.

[23]See John 10:10; John 8:12; Luke 19:10.

[24]See Matthew 10:34; Luke 12:49; Matthew 10:35; John 9:39.

[25]See Galatians 1:6-9; 1 Corinthians 10:1-13; 2 Peter 2:1; 1 John 2:18-27.

[26]"Repent, Repent, Anglicans Urged," *The Age,* accessed March 15, 2009, at <www.theage.com.au/news/national/repent-repent-anglicansurged/2006/03/31/1143441339520.html>.

[27]Ruth Powell and Kathy Jacka, *Moving Beyond Forty Years of Missing Generations,* NCLS Occasional Paper 10 (NCLS Research, January 2008); accessed March 15, 2009, at <www.ncls.org.au/default.aspx?sitemapid=6269>.

[28]Conversation with Colin Marshall, national director of the Ministry Training Scheme, November 26, 2005.

## CHAPTER 3: CONTAGIOUS RELATIONSHIPS

[1]Origen, "Against Celsus," *Ante-Nicene Fathers,* accessed March 13, 2009, at <www.ccel.org/ccel/schaff/anf04.toc.html>.

[2]Rodney Stark, *The Rise of Christianity: A Sociologist Reconsiders History* (Princeton, N.J.: Princeton University Press, 1996), p. 3.

[3]See Rodney Stark, *Cities of God: The Real Story of How Christianity Became an Urban Movement and Conquered Rome* (San Francisco: HarperSanFrancisco, 2006).

[4]Stark, *Rise of Christianity,* p. 208.

[5]Rodney Stark, *One True God: Historical Consequences of Monotheism* (Princeton, N.J.: Princeton University Press, 2001), p. 51.

[6]John Lofland and Rodney Stark, "Becoming a World-Saver: A Theory of Conversion to a Deviant Perspective," *American Sociological Review* 30 (1965): 862-75.

[7]See Luther P. Gerlach and Virginia H. Hine, *People, Power, Change: Movements of Social Transformation* (Indianapolis: Bobbs-Merrill, 1970), p. 97.

[8]See Stark, *Rise of Christianity,* pp. 20-22.

[9]Ibid., pp. 20, 193.

[10]Stark, *Cities of God*, p. 3. Following Arthur Darby Nock, *Conversion: The Old and the New in Religion from Alexander the Great to Augustine of Hippo* (Oxford: Clarendon, 1933), pp. 12, 13.

[11]See Gerlach and Hine, *People, Power, Change*, pp. 79-97.

[12]Ibid., p. 82.

[13]Lofland and Stark, "Becoming a World-Saver." See also David A. Snow, Louis A. Zurcher Jr. and Sheldon Ekland-Olson, "Social Networks and Social Movements: A Microstructural Approach to Differential Recruitment," *American Sociological Review* 45 (October 1980): 787-801.

[14]Gerlach and Hine, *People, Power, Change*, p. 97.

[15]Mark Granovetter, *Getting a Job: A Study of Contacts and Careers* (Chicago: University of Chicago Press, 1995).

[16]Malcolm Gladwell, *The Tipping Point: How Little Things Can Make a Big Difference* (London: Abacus, 2000), p. 51.

[17]Stark, "How New Religions Succeed," p. 23.

[18]Stark, *Rise of Christianity*, p. 20.

[19]Albert-Laszlo Barabasi, *Linked: How Everything Is Connected to Everything Else and What It Means* (New York: Plume, 2003), p. 30.

[20]Neil Cole, *Organic Church: Growing Faith Where Life Happens* (San Francisco: Jossey-Bass, 2005), p. 23.

[21]Ibid., p. 181.

**CHAPTER 4: RAPID MOBILIZATION**

[1]Frank Baker, *From Wesley to Asbury: Studies in Early American Methodism* (Durham, N.C.: Duke University Press, 1976), p. 118. Throughout this section I have relied on two sources: Roger Finke and Rodney Stark, "How the Upstart Sects Won America 1776-1850," *Journal for the Scientific Study of Religion* 28, no. 1 (March 1989): 27-44; and Roger Finke and Rodney Stark, *The Churching of America, 1776-1990: Winners and Losers in Our Religious Economy* (New Brunswick, N.J.: Rutgers University Press, 1992).

[2]See John H. Wigger, *Taking Heaven by Storm: Methodism and the Rise of Popular Christianity in America* (Urbana: University of Illinois Press, 1998), pp. 3-4; and Kenneth Scott Latourette, *The Great Century in Europe and the United States of America A.D. 1800-A.D. 1914*, vol. 4 of *A History of the Expansion of Christianity* (London: Eyre and Spottiswoode, 1941), p. 190.

[3]See Latourette, *Great Century*, p. 188.

[4]Wigger, *Taking Heaven by Storm*, pp. 21-22.

[5]Ibid., p. 11.

[6]Peter Cartwright, quoted in Finke and Stark, "Upstart Sects," p. 38.

[7]For the role of women and African Americans see Nathan O. Hatch, "The Puzzle of American Methodism," *Church History* 63 (1994): 175-89; and Wigger, *Taking Heaven by Storm*, pp. 123-72.

[8]Hatch, "Puzzle of American Methodism," pp. 178-79.

[9]Ibid., p. 179.

[10]Finke and Stark, "Upstart Sects," p. 42.

[11]Roland Allen, *The Spontaneous Expansion of the Church: And the Causes That Hinder It* (London: World Dominion Press, 1927), p. 126. See also Roland Allen, *Missionary Methods: St. Paul's Or Ours?* 4th ed. (London: World Dominion Press, 1912, 1956).

[12]Allen wrote, "Spontaneous zeal is alarming to them. When the faith is spread spontaneously both the charlatan and the saint find an opportunity for acquiring influence over others. Side by side with Peter is Simon Magus. In the working of an organization the man who is welcome and at home is the plain, mechanical, orderly man who will keep within the bounds. Not only the swindler but the inspired saint is a difficulty. He appears self-willed, extravagant, eccentric. He is independent and is always on the verge of breaking the orderly methods of the organization." Allen, *Spontaneous Expansion*, p. 148.

[13]Jenkins, *The Next Christendom*, p. 53.

[14]Ibid., p. 137.

[15]Eckhard Schnabel comments that "it is likely that the Twelve had a basic education. They did not come from the rural lower class but the vocational middle class. Pious families ensured their sons received, like Jesus, a good education in reading, writing and memorizing large amounts of scripture." Schnabel, *Early Christian Mission*, 1: 278.

[16]See Hans Küng, *The Church* (Garden City, N.Y.: Image Books, 1967), pp. 493-94.

[17]See E. Earle Ellis, "Paul and His Co-Workers," *New Testament Studies* 17 (1970-1971): 437-52.

[18]For travel and ministry with others see Acts 13:2, 13; 15:36-40; 16:1, 6; 18:18. For reference to fellow workers in letters see 2 Corinthians 1:1; Philippians 1:1; 2:19-30; Colossians 4:7-14. For sending team members on a mission see 1 Corinthians 4:17; 2 Corinthians 9:3; Ephesians 6:21-22; Philippians 2:19-30; Colossians 4:7-9.

[19]Sources for this section include personal conversations with Ralph Moore; Ralph Moore, *Let Go of the Ring: The Hope Chapel Story* (Honolulu: Straight Street Publishing, 2000); and Ralph Moore, *How to Multiply Your Church: The Most Effective Way to Grow God's Kingdom* (Ventura, Calif.: Regal, 2009).

## CHAPTER FIVE: ADAPTIVE METHODS

[1]For this section on William Carey I am indebted to Stephen Neill, *A History of Christian Missions*, Pelican History of the Church (Harmondsworth, U.K.: Penguin Books, 1964), pp. 261-65.

[2]Collins and Porras, *Built to Last*, p. 84.

[3]Peter F. Drucker, *Innovation and Entrepreneurship* (New York: HarperCollins, 1993), p. 192.

[4]See Thomas F. O'Dea, "Five Dilemmas of the Institutionalization of Religion," *Journal for the Scientific Study of Religion* 1, no. 1 (October 1961): 32. See also Bryan R. Wilson, *The Social Dimensions of Sectarianism: Sects and New Religious Movements in Contemporary Society* (Oxford: Clarendon, 1990), pp. 211-18.

[5]Wilson, *Social Dimensions of Sectarianism*, p. 212.

[6]See Eifion Evans, *The Welsh Revival of 1904* (Bryntirion: Evangelical Press of Wales, 1969).

[7]"What Is Alpha?" accessed March 7, 2009, at <http://uk.alpha.org>.

[8]"Translation Statistics," accessed March 15, 2009, at <www.wycliffe.org/About/Statistics.aspx>.

[9]"About Us," accessed March 23, 2009, at <www.storyrunners.com/about>.

[10]Lamin Sanneh, *Whose Religion Is Christianity? The Gospel Beyond the West* (Grand Rapids: Eerdmans, 2003), p. 69.

[11]See Jonathan J. Bonk, "The Defender of the Good News: Questioning Lamin Sanneh," *Christianity Today*, accessed April 9, 2009, at <www.christianity today.com/ct/2003/october/35.112.html>.

[12]See David A. Nadler and Mark B. Nadler, "The Success Syndrome: Why Established Market Leaders Usually Stumble—and What You Can Do to Prevent It," *Leader to Leader* 7 (Winter 1998): 43-50.

[13]See Collins and Porras, *Built to Last*.

[14]See Schnabel, *Early Christian Mission*, 1:295.

[15]See Birger Gerhardsson, *Origins of the Gospel Traditions* (London: SCM Press, 1979), pp. 67-77.

[16]See Schnabel, *Early Christian Mission*, 1:242-47.

[17]See Eckhard J. Schnabel, *Early Christian Mission*, vol. 2, *Paul and the Early Church* (Downers Grove, Ill.: IVP Academic, 2004), p. 1546.

[18]See Schnabel's comments on 1 Corinthians 9:19-23 in *Early Christian Mission*, 2:953-60.

[19]Ibid., p. 1337.

[20]Latourette, *A History of the Expansion of Christianity*, 1:165.

[21]See David Garrison, *Church Planting Movements: How God Is Redeeming a Lost World* (Midlothian, Va.: WIGTake Resources, 2004). See also David

Garrison, "Church Planting Movements" <http://churchplantingmove ments.com/download.php>.

## CONCLUSION: THE FUTURE IS ALREADY HERE

[1]David B. Barrett, Todd M. Johnson, and Peter F. Crossing, "Missiometrics 2008: Reality Checks for Christian World Communions," *International Bulletin of Missionary Research* 32, no. 1 (January 2008): 28-30.

[2]Philip Jenkins, *God's Continent: Christianity, Islam and Europe's Religious Crisis* (New York: Oxford University Press, 2009), pp. 74-75, following David B. Barrett, George T. Kurian and Todd M. Johnson, *World Christian Encyclopedia: A Comparative Survey of Churches and Religions in the Modern World*, 2nd ed. (New York: Oxford University Press, 2001), pp. 12-15.

[3]Jenkins, *God's Continent*, pp. 87-89.

[4]Michael Luo, "Preaching the Word and Quoting the Voice," *New York Times*, February 26, 2006.

[5]See Bob Roberts Jr., *The Multiplying Church: The New Math for Starting New Churches* (Grand Rapids: Zondervan, 2008).

# LIKEWISE. *Go and do.*

A man comes across an ancient enemy, beaten and left for dead. He lifts the wounded man onto the back of a donkey and takes him to an inn to tend to the man's recovery. Jesus tells this story and instructs those who are listening to "go and do likewise."

Likewise books explore a compassionate, active faith lived out in real time. When we're skeptical about the status quo, Likewise books challenge us to create culture responsibly. When we're confused about who we are and what we're supposed to be doing, Likewise books help us listen for God's voice. When we're discouraged by the troubled world we've inherited, Likewise books encourage us to hold onto hope.

In this life we will face challenges that demand our response. Likewise books face those challenges with us so we can act on faith.

*likewisebooks.com*